*Awash with tears, I choked out,
"All I can see is my little boy, all alone
on the side of that hill,
buried six feet under the ground,
and the water is falling . . .
and is hitting him . . . and hitting him . . .
and I can't do anything to protect him."*

*I suddenly felt like a caged lion,
desperate to get out.
"I want to get a shovel and go dig him up
and bring him home and put him
in our back yard. I'm his father,
and I want to protect him."*

*Peggy just looked at me,
her eyes full of understanding.
She didn't say a word.*

Foreword by T. Ray Rachels

We'll Never Forget You, JJ

Don and Peggy Gregg
with Don Tanner

UPLIFT BOOKS

We'll Never Forget You, JJ

© 1990 by Don and Peggy Gregg

Published by
UPLIFT BOOKS
26422 Dracaea Ave.
Moreno Valley, CA 92360

Library of Congress Cataloging-in-Publication Data
Gregg, Donald Leon, 1951-
    We'll never forget you, JJ : handling the loss of a loved one /
by Donald Leon Gregg and Peggy Sue Gregg with Don Tanner.
       p. cm.
   ISBN 0-88005-005-5 : $8.95
    1. Bereavement — Psychological aspects. 2. Children — Death —
Psychological aspects. 3. Brothers and sisters — Death — Psycho-
logical aspects. 4. Parent and child. 5. Consolation. 6. Gregg,
Jacob.   I. Gregg, Peggy Sue, 1951-   II. Tanner, Don.
III. Title.
BF575.G7G72   1990   90-12245
155.9'.37--dc20   CIP

Printed in the United States of America

TO
Braxton and Donny
and
Bethany Church of Alhambra
with love

Contents

Acknowledgments

To Don Tanner who faithfully and skillfully assisted us with the writing of this book. Thank you for your patience and gentle spirit in helping us smooth a lot of rough edges. Also to Jean Bryant who shared in presenting our message. Thank you for your special expertise in the writing and editing process.

To Joan York who was always willing, always kind, for the many hours she spent transcribing interview tapes. And to Donna Lewicki who helped in the transcribing. We give thanks.

To Darlene Weaver who listened to and walked through a lot of painful areas with us, our deep gratitude. Thank you for your compassionate heart.

To Blake and Esther Gibbs who have given us the confidence we feel in sharing ourselves. Your love, support and friendship created a safe place for us. Thank you for sharing with us the experience of unconditional love.

To Bob, Bobby and Heather Cave and Betty Pelc, our "extended family," who were a special part of Jacob's life from the beginning. Thank you for the memories that will forever bind us together.

To Don and Marilyn Shaffer, Dominic and Jean Palermo, Tom and Darlene Weaver, Oogie and Donna Schmidt, and Ruth Cobb who are very special people in our lives. We are truly thankful that you have continued to keep the memory of Jacob alive.

To our families who have all grown through the pain. We are grateful for you.

To Bethany Church of Alhambra who have loved us and loved us and loved us. We feel privileged to be associated with such a Christ-centered fellowship. Thank you.

Foreword

This story is for every parent whose young child has put the imprint of love on his or her heart. Don and Peggy Gregg's account of their six-year-old son Jacob's tragic death, their coping with the awesome realities of losing him, and the hard work of rebuilding their family's shattered dreams has put human life onto its most elementary and meaningful levels.

The broken heart of sudden loss is felt very strongly in Don and Peggy's remembrances, yet there is a glory that breathes through the lines giving much more significance than just a quick look into what happened to little Jacob.

Other questions—far deeper than, "Why was Jacob taken so suddenly and so soon?"—are raised and answered with a natural ease, possible only because it was born out of the Greggs' bedrock faith in God.

"The Lord gives and the Lord takes away; blessed be the Name of the Lord!" was Job's chest-heaving lament—and his affirmation of the goodness of the Lord as well—following the news of great losses in his family.

The comfort, understanding and response of our earthly family and friends are of tremendous value during times of crisis; but when the storms of life bring us face to face with this kind of grief, Jesus Christ is life's best refuge. And it is the Gregg family's relationship with Jesus—and their own affirmation of the goodness of God—that puts this book into its broadest perspective.

I was a neighboring pastor to Don and Peggy when the news of Jacob's accident came. Word of the tragedy spread quickly and by the time of the funeral, Bethany Church was filled with not only those from the Alhambra congregation, but long lines of mourners from our ministerial fraternity as well.

11

Most of us take the blows life hands us, tuck them away, unable to do anything else, and go on to work through our grief alone. Don and Peggy have documented their struggle with one of life's deepest wounds and brought forth their triumphant story with a courage and inspiration that far transcends the wound itself. Such a recounting, difficult as it must have been, is a remarkable gift of love to all of us who have lost anyone very dear.

When Peggy was at wits end during those days, God brought to her the Bible verse: "The God of Jacob is our refuge." With it He provided the essential grip on divine love she needed at the time. It is this revelation of the goodness of God as a refuge that holds us all.

For myself, I can only say thank you for that great gift, and I feel confident that after you read this story, you'll have a thank you all your own to say.

T. Ray Rachels
District Superintendent
Southern California District
Assemblies of God

A Child of Mine

I'll lend you, for a little time,
   a child of Mine, He said,
For you to love the while he lives,
   and mourn for when he's dead.

It may be three or seven years,
   or twenty-two or three,
But will you, 'til I call him back,
   take care of him for Me?

He'll bring his charms to gladden you,
   and should his stay be brief,
You'll have his lovely memories
   as solace for your grief.

I cannot promise he will stay,
   since all from earth return,
But there are lessons taught down there
   I want this child to learn.

I've looked the wide world over
   in search for teachers true,
And from the throngs that crowd life's lanes,
   I have selected you.

Now will you give him all your love,
   nor think the labor vain,
Nor hate Me, when I come to call
   to take him back again?

13

I fancied that I heard them say,
  Dear Lord, Thy will be done!
For all the joys Thy child shall bring,
  the risk of grief we'll run.

We'll shelter him with tenderness;
  we'll love him while we may,
And for the happiness we've known,
  forever grateful stay.

But should the angels call for him
  much sooner than we've planned,
We'll brave the bitter grief that comes —
  and try to understand.

—Author unknown

We'll Never Forget You, JJ

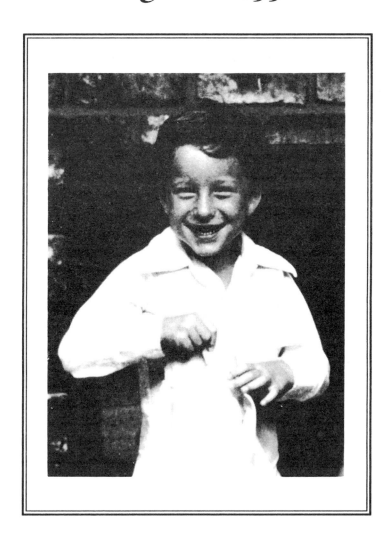

1

Fast Trip to San Diego

"Don, I have some bad news for you. Are you sitting down?"

I stiffened when I heard the somber voice of my associate pastor, Tom Benton, on the telephone. "What is it?"

"Jacob's been in an accident, and . . . "

"How bad?" I interrupted, tightening my grip on the receiver.

"Well, I don't know, but it doesn't look good. He's in surgery."

"Where's Peggy?"

"She's here right now," Tom answered — too quietly. "Where are you?"

"I'm calling from a pay phone. I got hung up in traffic and had to stop for gas. I'll be there as fast as I can."

Stunned by the news, I dropped the telephone receiver into its cradle and raced toward my car. *How can this be happening to us? After all we've done for God, the least He can do is protect our children!*

I arrived at the church thirty minutes later. Peggy's mother, father and sister were waiting with my church staff. Peggy had given the hospital in San Diego permission to operate on our six-year-old son, Jacob.

Peggy and I had taken Jacob and his older brother, Braxton, down to visit their grandparents in San Diego after the evening service the preceding Sunday. Early this afternoon, Wednesday, the boys had been visiting my brother David and his wife Gracia. The boys had gone bike riding, and Jacob had been struck by a car and had suffered a head injury. No one at that moment knew how serious it was.

I called Grossmont Hospital, where Jacob had been taken, to find out what was going on. They put my father on the phone.

"Don, the doctors are doing everything they can for Jacob, but they won't know how he's going to be until after surgery," he assured me. "All I know is that there is some swelling in Jacob's brain. They'll tell us more later on."

"Peggy and I are on our way," I said anxiously.

Our minister of youth, Bob Cave, rode with us to San Diego. Peggy's mother and father followed an hour later. Little was said as we snaked our way through the rush-hour freeway traffic. I wept inwardly, trying not to show Peggy what I was feeling. She prayed quietly and occasionally exchanged comments with Bob.

Suddenly, just as we were passing Angel Stadium in Anaheim, I felt a familiar presence in the car. No visible appearance nor audible voice could have been more real. My perception was that of Jacob beside me with his little hand on my shoulder saying, "It's okay, Dad. I'm gone, but it's okay."

A strange mixture of hopelessness and calm crept over me, and I was almost oblivious to the heavy traffic around me. Although everything about Jacob's condition at that point was speculative, I knew in my spirit that he had gone to be with the Lord.

Jacob loved baseball. It seemed appropriate that the Lord would choose the moment we were passing the stadium to let me know that Jacob was gone. How should I break the news to Peggy? I remained alone with the experience, not wanting to say anything until my feelings were confirmed.

Finally, I could take the pain of suspense no longer. Pulling off the freeway to a fast-food restaurant, I ran inside and placed a call to the hospital. My father picked up the phone in the emergency room.

"Jacob has just come out of surgery. The situation is critical," he said somberly. "The doctors have told us that there's no sign of brain activity, and they're going to transfer Jacob to Donald Sharp Hospital where the trauma team will take over."

I now knew that what I had sensed in the car was real. The Lord had indeed begun to prepare me for Jacob's death. I stood there a moment and pondered the irony of the situation. Our precious son, surviving only on a life-support system, was being transferred to die in the very same hospital he was born in just six years, nine months and seventeen days earlier. Furthermore, I remembered that Sharp Hospital also performed organ transplants. I walked slowly back to the car, knowing we would soon have to face the decision of whether or not Jacob would become a donor.

Bob met me part way between the restaurant and the car. "How is he?" he asked quietly.

"He's dead . . . "

Peggy, who had been waiting in the car, read my lips and burst open the door. "Don't say that! Don't say that," she screamed angrily. "He's not dead!" In shock, trying to escape the truth, she began running aimlessly across the parking lot, with Bob and me in pursuit.

This was not the first time Peggy had reacted this way, and I knew we were in trouble. On an earlier occasion Donny, our youngest son, had been running a high fever and his body went into convulsions, leaving him partially paralyzed. As we rushed him to the hospital, he stopped breathing and began to turn blue. All the while, Peggy was screaming and I was trying to calm her down.

As we pulled up in front of the emergency room, Peggy burst the car door open and dashed into the hospital yelling, "My baby is dying! My baby is dying!" A nurse grabbed Donny and ran toward an examining table, and Peggy dropped to her knees and sobbed, "Jesus, help him, help him!"

With the news now that Jacob was dead, I was not surprised when Peggy lost control. Bob and I caught up with her and finally managed to calm her down enough to get her back to the car, and we again headed for San Diego.

The rest of the drive was quiet as I tried to find the right words to tell my wife what I knew. I also wrestled with the idea of Jacob being a transplant donor. Finally, I broke the silence.

"Honey, there are some things we need to look at if Jacob is not going to make it," I began cautiously, explaining why I believed Jacob was being transferred to Sharp Hospital. "We're probably going to be asked to make some decisions about him being a transplant donor . . ."

"I don't want to hear that! You don't know if that's why they took him there! We'll just have to see! I don't even want to talk about it!"

"We don't have to deal with it now, honey," I answered tenderly, "but we need to be thinking about it. We're going to be asked to make some tough decisions, and . . . "

"What does *that* mean?" she blurted. "Are you just giving up? God can do something for us. We've got to hang on longer than this!"

Finally, after nearly three hours on the road, we arrived at Sharp Hospital—just in time to see the ambulance bringing Jacob to the emergency entrance. As the ambulance attendants wheeled Jacob into the emergency room on a stretcher, we rushed into the hospital.

My father met us at the door. "Donny, talk to David," he said deliberately. "The family is so worried. It was just an accident."

"I don't care how it happened, I'm only concerned about Jacob!" I answered quickly, handing my ring full of keys to my mother. "Here, Mom, put these in your purse." Peggy and I dashed past the rest of our waiting family toward the emergency room.

We pushed open the door and started to enter. "You can't come in here!" a surgical nurse objected firmly. Beyond her we could see several doctors and other members of the trauma team working on Jacob.

"We're the parents, and we haven't seen our son," I explained to the nurse, hoping she would let us in.

"Not now," she insisted. "We have to stabilize him from the transfer across town first and get him hooked up to the life-support equipment."

"When *can* we see him?" I pressed.

"You'll have to give us at least an hour. So, if you'll just wait over there," she suggested kindly, pointing to the waiting area where our family had gathered, "we'll come and tell you when you can see your boy."

That next hour was the longest of our lives. Over and over again, we asked questions of my parents and my brother and sister-in-law, David and Gracia, trying to find out exactly what had happened.

Jacob and Braxton had been playing with their cousins, Brooks and Casey. Jacob, Braxton and Casey had decided to ride their bicycles in a vacant lot down the hill from David and Gracia's home. When they arrived, Braxton noticed that one of Jacob's tires seemed to be flat and he was having trouble riding it. He sent Jacob back to get the tire fixed.

David and Gracia's home is on an incline. Jacob apparently didn't make it up the steep driveway the first time and was coasting down the driveway to take another shot at the hill. Just as he entered the street, a car screeched its brakes and swerved in a futile attempt to miss him. Thrown sixteen feet by the impact, Jacob landed on the back of his head.

When Jacob didn't return, Braxton went to get him. On his way back, Braxton saw an ambulance and a crowd in front of the house. Curious, he pushed his way through the crowd — and saw Jacob lying on the street, unconscious. Paramedics were checking his vital signs. Picking up Jacob's shoe, Braxton ran up the driveway to tell his aunt — and call his mother.

Peggy _____

When the phone rang at our home, I was just on my way out the door. Donny was in preschool, and this was to be my first day back in school as a student since Don and I were married. At first, I wasn't going to pick up the phone. *If it's important, they'll call back,* I thought. But something told me to answer it.

"Mom, Jacob's been hit by a car. But he's okay. He's just a little bit unconscious, and there was hardly any blood." By the tone of Braxton's voice, I didn't think the accident was serious. "They just took him to the hospital, and they're going to check him out. Papaw [Braxton's grandfather] will probably be calling you."

"Okay, baby, thank you for calling. You did the right thing," I soothed. "Mommy and Daddy will be down there in just a little bit."

The seriousness of the accident didn't begin to dawn on me until Tom Benton came to the door. I fully expected Don and I would drive to San Diego and bring Jacob home.

"There's been an accident," Tom said soberly as I opened the door.

"I know. I just talked to Braxton."

"Sit down, Peggy," he motioned to the couch. "Let's pray together." All the while he prayed, I wondered why Tom was more serious than usual. Moments later, we left for the church. I became more frightened when my mother and sister arrived at the church crying. I began to panic when we couldn't reach Don. By the time the hospital in San Diego phoned to get permission to operate on Jacob, my stomach was tied in such painful knots that I had to lean over the desk while talking to the nurse. Finally, Don arrived, and we left for the hospital.

Once we got there, we had to wait while the trauma team got Jacob stabilized, and the time seemed endless. Gracia had taken Braxton to the home of one of her friends, and I called to see how he was. She put him on the phone.

"Mom, how's Jacob?" he asked.

"I don't know, honey. Daddy and I just got here. They're working on him, and I'll call you right after we get to see him," I assured him.

"Well, Mommy, I'm praying for him, and I'm holding his shoe."

I struggled hard against the lump in my throat to say something more to encourage Braxton, but could barely get the words out to say goodbye.

Two weeks before the accident, I had a feeling that something tragic was going to happen to our family. I had shared this premonition with Betty Pelc, a young woman who lived with us. While attending a General Council of the Assemblies of God a few days later, Betty called to let us know that one of our church members had been in an automobile accident and had broken almost every bone in her body.

"Do you think that's the tragedy I've been feeling would come?" I asked Betty, hoping for reassurance. "Do you think it was a church family member instead of one of our own family?"

"I don't know, Peggy."

"It's funny. I still have the feeling . . . but this must be it," I had said.

Then the premonition faded from my memory — until now. Had this been the Lord's way of preparing me for Jacob's death?

Standing in the hallway of the intensive care unit and trying desperately to keep my sanity, I directed all my remaining energy inward. I watched the mouths of those waiting with us move as they talked to me, but I wasn't hearing a word they were saying. Suddenly, my eyes riveted on Gracia. Outwardly, she is not an emotional person; her feelings run deep. I sensed that beneath her crying she desperately needed reassuring that we did not blame her for the accident. I stepped across the room and slipped my arms around her.

"Gracia, we love you very much and know that you care for our boys as much as you care for your own children," I comforted. "The accident could have happened in front of our house. We don't blame you for what happened. There wasn't anything you could have done to prevent it."

She didn't reply. I prayed that somehow my words would ease her pain.

Meanwhile, Don managed to get his father and brother alone down the hallway so he could learn what they knew of Jacob's condition. Finally, the doctor stepped through the emergency room door and entered the waiting room. Silently, without breathing, we waited for him to tell us the news.

2

Sweet Dreams of Jesus

Don _____

The doctor looked at us as kindly as he could. His voice was deliberate but compassionate. "Jacob, for all intents and purposes, is dead," he said slowly. "His heart is still beating with the help of a life-support system, but his brain is dead."

Peggy and I looked at each other for a moment, communicating with our eyes how much we loved and needed each other. We each silently made an instant, deep commitment to the other, to be supportive and to help each other get through this experience, no matter what happened. The weeping of our family and friends who had gathered to be with us seemed lost in the intensely personal moment that she and I shared. We fell into each other's arms and hugged tightly.

As we finished our embrace, we turned toward the doctor. "How much time will we have with Jacob?" I asked quietly.

He shook his head. "We cannot keep him going indefinitely. Within two to three hours the swelling in his brain will cause the flow of blood to be shut off and his heart will stop. We can't control the swelling."

"Can we see him?" I choked.

"Yes."

Hand in hand, Peggy and I walked slowly and steadily into the Intensive Care Unit to spend what little time we had with our precious son. As I caught sight of Jacob, the reality of his death which I had experienced on the way to the hospital seemed to escape me. My mind searched for a promise that I could make to God, or some deal that He might find acceptable, so He would spare my boy's life.

"Let's pray," I whispered to Peggy. "Maybe God can do something for him . . . "

Peggy _____

I could not accept Jacob's death until the moment we entered the room and saw him lying on the bed connected to the life-support apparatus. Suddenly a mental picture formed in my mind of Jesus standing at Jacob's bedside with His arms outstretched. It was as though the Lord were giving me a choice. I could place Jacob in His arms, or He could reach down and take him. I chose to pick our son up and place him in Jesus' arms. I cannot describe the peace that flooded my heart at that moment, but it was the same peace that the apostle wrote about in Philippians 4:7: "You will experience God's peace, which is far more wonderful than the human mind can understand. His peace will keep your thoughts and your hearts quiet and at rest as you trust in Christ Jesus" (TLB).

For the next two hours, Don and I held Jacob's hand. We rubbed his little arms and we kissed his face and hands repeatedly. Our awareness that he was truly gone didn't stop us from showering our love upon this little boy who had brought so much happiness into our lives. We spoke words of love into his ear as we bonded in our commitment to release him. I bent over his cold, pale body and whispered, "Sweet dreams of Jesus," which I had done often when I put Jacob to bed.

Meanwhile, we were not alone. Other children were in the Intensive Care Unit, and members of our family and friends periodically slipped into the room to see Jacob.

Don

With each kiss and with each word that we spoke to Jacob, I became more resigned to his death. How foolish I had been to think that God wanted a promise or would make a deal. I realized that my son was in a situation that his daddy had no control over, and I was going to have to release him into the tender care of our Lord. Technically, the life-support system was keeping him alive, but his spirit had already left this piece of clay that we call a body.

I gazed at his frail form for a moment — so pale that I could hardly see his little freckles — then bent low over his cold body. "We love you," I whispered into his ear. "We'll see you again. Sweet dreams of Jesus."

Tears coursing down my cheeks, I lifted my head and looked around the room at the other children. They were in life-and-death situations. Was there anything we could do to help them? The moment of decision had come. Would Jacob would become a transplant donor?

For years I had been repulsed by the idea that any member of my family could become a donor. We came into this world with all our parts, I reasoned, and to the best of my ability we would go out with all our pieces. Still, my heart reached out to those desperately suffering children, and donating a part of Jacob so that others might have a chance to live seemed the most natural thing to do. I sought out the doctor, and we discussed the procedures.

"As soon as you decide, and give us permission, we'll have the coroner come over here to pronounce him dead," the doctor explained. "Then we will take him into the operating room."

"Are you going to unhook him?" I asked. "We want to be with him when you do."

"Well, that won't be possible because we can't unhook your son until we get him into the operating room and actually remove the organs," the doctor refused. "If we do anything sooner, the organs will be damaged, and we won't be able to use them."

"How long before the coroner gets here?"

"About a half hour."

"Could we spend some time alone with him then?"

"Yes, of course."

We decided to donate Jacob's kidneys and corneas. One kidney would go to a diabetic man in Oregon who was married and the father of two children; the other would be given to a young woman in Texas who had been on dialysis for a year. Jacob's corneas would be used to help restore the sight of a twelve-year-old boy in San Diego.

I asked, "What about his heart?"

"I'm sorry," the doctor answered. "We've had to give him dopamine all along, and other medications, and they've just been too damaging to his heart. We can't use it for a transplant." Again, he said, "I'm sorry."

As we talked, a nurse asked us to sign release papers. "Now you understand that when they go in, they're going to take his eyes out," she informed.

Peggy turned to me in disbelief. "I can't believe they're doing this to my baby," she cried. "No way can they do that!"

Sympathetically, the nurse withdrew the form. "No problem. We won't do it. We won't even talk about it."

"Isn't there another way to remove the corneas?" I probed.

"Yes, they can remove the cornea without removing the eyeball, but it's more difficult," she explained.

"If they can, please do that," we requested.

Once the arrangements were made and the release was signed, I placed a long distance call to our church to let the staff know of Jacob's passing and ask someone to bring our three-year-old son, Donny, to the hospital. He was already on the way.

It was time to call Braxton to the hospital as well. As soon as the boys arrived, we would explain to them that Jacob was gone and say our goodbyes as a family before the transplant operation began.

Peggy and I spent the next few minutes alone with Jacob, holding each other's hands and reminiscing over past times with him. We wondered how we would tell Braxton and Donny, and whether we should let them see Jacob.

Finally, Donny arrived with two of our staff members. Braxton came, too—still holding Jacob's shoe, which he had not let go of since the accident. His cousins, Casey and Brooks, were with him.

As Braxton entered the waiting room where the family had gathered, he called to Peggy. "Mom, where's Jakie? Is he looking for his shoe? I've brought his shoe. How is he?" The cheer in his voice sounded forced as he sought to reassure himself, but none of us could say anything.

The words lodged in my throat as I tried to tell him about Jacob. Sensing my great difficulty, my brother David came to the rescue. He escorted the children into another room. Then, taking Donny on his lap, he began to tell them what happened.

"Jacob has gone to be with Jesus," he explained gently. "We were hoping everything would work out, but he died."

Donny sat quietly, not fully understanding what his Uncle David was saying.

But Braxton understood. He had come to the hospital fully expecting to see Jacob sitting up in bed eating ice cream. Returning with the others to the waiting room—still holding Jacob's shoe—he threw his arms around us and started to cry and tell us how much he loved us.

I cannot put into words the sense of loss that I saw in Braxton's eyes. It was like he lost his innocence, like he felt betrayed. Though the words were never spoken, his eyes were agonizing, "But, Dad, they told me he was okay. Dad, how come?"

As we hugged, I sensed he needed me to hold him tight, to feel secure in my arms.

He was full of fearful questions. "What did the doctors say? Why didn't the operation work? Why can't they do another operation? What are we going to do now?"

We knew immediately that we dared not let the scars of this tragedy crust over Braxton's tender heart. So whatever he asked, we tried to answer as truthfully and openly as possible.

"Accidents are beyond our control," we assured him. "If it is Jacob's time to go, there is nothing anyone can do to stop that."

Knowing that Braxton was a sensitive boy and particularly vulnerable at this time, we were hesitant to let him see Jacob. Even so, we felt it was best that he did.

Braxton screamed when he saw Jacob, then ran over and threw his arms around his brother. Peggy tried to pry him away, but Braxton held on tighter, sobbing.

"Don! Let's get him out. Let's just get him out!" Peggy cried.

"No. Wait," I motioned.

"Get him out, Don. Get him out!"

"No, just let him alone," I persisted. Knowing that down the road this would be a special memory for Braxton, I wanted to give him these final moments to say anything he wanted to Jacob.

After a few minutes, Braxton grew quieter, and we began to pray as a family, thanking God for lending Jacob to us and for the joy that he had brought into our lives.

"Thank you, Lord, for entrusting Jacob's preparation for Heaven to our care. We remember the covenant we made to You on the day of his dedication, that we would do our best to prepare Jacob for Heaven and freely give him up when You call for him — on the condition that when we get to Heaven, we can take him back.

"Help us, Lord, to carry through with that dedication, which we said with our mouths and must now seal with our lives. Help us not to allow Jakie's death to rob us of that commitment, for it was made from our hearts because of the joy that You had given to us.

"He's Your child, God, not ours. We trusted You with him when he was alive, and we will trust You with him now that he is gone. We will trust you with our other children as well. Amen."

By this time the operating room was ready and the trauma team was standing by. I tugged gently at Braxton. "It's time to go, honey," I said quietly.

"Daddy, I don't want to go," he whimpered.

"You need to release Jacob," I tugged again. "He's not here anymore."

Slowly, reluctantly, he finally let go of Jacob, but he still gripped his shoe.

My mother and father took Braxton and Donny home with them, where we would join them later for the night. Meanwhile, we waited at the hospital while the transplant surgery was performed. We talked about Jacob, and we laughed and we cried as we spoke of all that he meant to us. As the hours passed, I encouraged the others who had remained with us to go home. There was nothing more they could do. One by one, each of them hugged us, spoke a word of love and encouragement, and left. Dallas Miller, a close family friend and a pastor in San Diego, stayed until the transplant operation was over, then with a word of prayer, he left too.

Peggy and I were alone for the first time since we had arrived at the hospital.

Slowly, we made our way one more time to Jacob's side. The machines were all unhooked. He looked so peaceful, so angelic, so much at rest, that it took some of the hurt away. With one last kiss, we stepped out of the room and down the hall to the front of the hospital, then out to our car for the twenty-minute drive to my parent's home. And into a life without our middle son.

3

Peace in the Storm

As we walked wearily toward our car, arm in arm, I peered at my watch — barely able to see the dial in the early morning darkness. *Two o'clock!* I had lost track of time. Although exhausted, sleep seemed far from our minds.

I took my arm away from Peggy and reached into my pocket for the car keys. My pocket was empty!

"I can't believe it!" I exclaimed.

"What's the matter?" Peggy yawned.

"I don't have my keys! I gave them to my mom when we came to the hospital because they were too bulky to put in my pocket. Now we're stranded."

Suddenly, both of us started laughing, expecting any moment to break into tears. We strode back to the hospital to call my parents, only to discover that we were locked out. The glass doors opened out, and no one could enter through them. That day the worst thing in the world had happened to us, and now this. What else could go wrong?

I looked up into the sky to check whether or not God was still in control.

We began pounding on the door to attract someone's attention. We could see three nurses inside scurrying between their work station and patient rooms attending to various chores, but they could not see us. Feeling numb, helpless and abandoned — even by God — we continued to bang on the door until one of them finally heard us and came to see what was wrong.

"I don't have the keys to my car," I explained quickly. "May I use your telephone?"

"Yes, of course!" the nurse nodded kindly, opening the door. "You can use the one in there." She pointed to a nearby office.

Nervously, I dialed my father's number.

"Dad, I've got some great news for you," I announced facetiously when he answered.

"What's that?"

"I don't have my car keys. You're going to have to pick us up."

"Where are they?"

"I gave them to Mom and forgot to get them from her when you left. So we don't have any way to get home. And we can't stay here very much longer . . . "

"I'll be right there."

A nurse brought us some coffee while Peggy and I waited in the lobby. Perplexing questions troubled our minds, and we talked. Where was God when our son needed Him? Why didn't He protect Jacob? Why did He allow Braxton to discover his brother unconscious on the street, where a crowd of curious bystanders had already gathered to watch the paramedics attend to his still form? Why did the accident have to happen while Jacob was in the care of relatives? I shuddered at the thought of the potential problems that could arise in our family over this.

My sense of loneliness deepened as we contemplated our situation. Even so, God had not abandoned us. In those moments when I thought we had been forgotten, God was showing that He did indeed, as the psalmist said, "sit King upon the flood." We felt tossed in the floodwater of our sorrow, but God was taking us into His wonderful hands and stabilizing us with His precious Holy Spirit.

We were keenly aware of the kindness and concern shown to our family while Jacob was still at Grossmont Hospital. The staff had done everything possible to help alleviate the pressure my mom and dad and brother and sister-in-law were feeling. They had kept them informed of every detail of Jacob's condition, and had assisted them in making the necessary decisions about his care until we arrived.

When my father arrived, my cousins George and Sharon were with him. They had just learned of the accident and were at his home when I called.

"Do you want to see Jacob?" I asked weakly.

George and Sharon glanced at each other, not knowing what to say. Hesitantly, they nodded yes.

As we stepped slowly toward the recovery room where Peggy and I had last seen Jacob, I began to think of his injuries, particularly his swollen eye, and imagine how he would look during the funeral. Their reaction would determine whether we should have an open or a closed casket. If they were shocked, I would have the casket closed. Apprehensively, I tried to prepare them.

"Jakie had some bruising on his hip and arms and some scratches on his back, but most of the damage was done to the back part of his head," I began. "He also has some swelling on his right eye and bruises underneath the eye and around his lips. His head was shaved, and he's wearing a bandage that looks a little like a turban . . . "

They listened quietly, gently trying to calm my fears as I continued to describe Jacob's condition.

"He's not too ugly to look at," I assured, "but now that death has set in, I'm wondering if it won't make him look worse."

We arrived at the door of the recovery room, and I knocked once, twice, three times — but no one answered.

"Maybe I'd better go in first," I offered, "to make sure it's okay for you to come in."

I determined to take one last look at Jacob to make sure everything was all right. The recovery room was set with several beds with little curtains around them. After the transplant surgery, Jacob had been taken into a small, sterile room within the recovery area. Surrounded by wired windows, the room contained only one bed and some medical apparatus. I wanted to make sure he was still there.

Finding the recovery room empty of patients and nurses, I stepped quickly toward the little room. I was not prepared for what I saw. Someone had placed a rubber surgeon's glove on Jacob's head, the fingers covering most of his face.

"How could they do this to my baby?" I muttered between clenched teeth.

Every uncaring thing that I had ever imagined that could go on in a hospital after a family leaves their loved one seemed to come true at this moment. *When they think you're gone, they just walk out and leave their glove on your boy!* I smirked, jerking it off his face. *How could they be so insensitive! If they had to cover his face, why couldn't they just put a sheet over it, or a wash cloth?*

I've always been a person who likes to be in control. If I can't control a situation, at least I want to know the direction in which it's going. At this moment, everything seemed to be slipping through my fingers, and I was feeling so inadequate as a father. I hadn't been here to protect my son, and what could I say now? There was no one to yell at. And if I did, what good would it do?

In my haste, I didn't notice the coldness of the glove. Suddenly, I realized that it was filled with ice. Feeling a twinge of shame, I peered at Jacob's face. The swelling that had closed his eye was gone. Now a bandage could cover his little head so that others would be able to view him one final time.

Only then did I begin to see that the keys and this second trip into the recovery room were not accidents, that God was taking away my fears of how Jacob would look at the funeral. He knew that an open or closed casket would become a big concern to me. By allowing us to become stranded and by the many courtesies that had been shown to us by the hospital staff, God was letting me know that He was still in control. Though I doubted it, He was going to take care of us.

Gently, I laid the glove back on Jacob's head and covered it again with the small skull cap the nurses had placed over it. I started to leave, then stopped. *What if this hits Peggy like it did me? Better take it off again. I'll just make sure to replace it when we all leave so the swelling will stay down.* And that's what I did, so the ice could continue its work.

After the others all viewed Jacob, we once again made our way to the cars. Dad drove our car with Peggy in front, and I sat in the back.

Most of the ride was quiet as we all tried to put things into perspective. Lost in the depths of our individual hurts, each of us hoped another would break the tense silence. Even so, our feelings were deeper than words could surface. In such times, only the Holy Spirit can speak the unutterable groanings of our heart.

Suddenly, Peggy began to pray in her heavenly language. Startled at first, I quickly realized she was sharing her deepest anguish and the Holy Spirit was interceding for us all.

The apostle Paul speaks of this inward groaning in Romans 8 and says, "The Spirit also helps our weakness; for we do not know how to pray as we should, but the Spirit Himself intercedes for us with groanings too deep for words; He who searches the hearts knows what the mind of the Spirit is, because He intercedes for the saints according to the will of God." In that context, Paul said, "And we know that God causes all things to work together for good to those who love God, to those who are called according to His purpose." How God would work Jacob's death for our good, I did not know. I did know that the Holy Spirit was taking our case to the Father. He, better than we, could share the depths of the pain we were feeling, and He could bring back the answer from Heaven for us in due time.

As Peggy prayed in the Spirit, an abiding peace entered our car. All the tenseness and uncertainty of the moment vanished. I remembered when Jesus' disciples were crossing the Sea of Galilee and a fierce storm arose.

What a triumphant moment when Jesus rose to His feet and rebuked the winds and the sea! It was no less awesome to me that our storm became calm.

This incident was the first of many similar experiences that Peggy would have in the weeks and months to come as she struggled through her grief. Often the Holy Spirit would wrap His loving arms around her when human comfort would fail. Even now God was releasing peace and inner strength that I never thought she possessed.

Braxton and Donny were fast asleep on the sofa bed in the family room when we arrived. Peggy and I slid quietly into the bed, each taking one of the boys and hugging him. With their heads cradled in our arms, and Braxton still holding Jacob's shoe, we settled down for the rest of the night.

For me, sleep seemed elusive. As the moments ticked slowly by, I could hear the rhythmic breathing of my sleeping family. Our children were the most important things in our lives. We spent a lot of time with them. In my mind I kept seeing Jacob in different stages of his life. I remembered when he was born, his first steps, his first words, his first bike, what a great baseball and soccer player he was, how much he loved the Lord . . .

4

Never Say "Can't"

"Isn't he the most beautiful baby you have ever seen?" Peggy cooed for the second time.

I smiled as I remembered those joyful words. Jacob was born on November 14, 1976. He was not by any stretch of the imagination a beautiful baby. Cute maybe, but not beautiful.

Walking into Peggy's hospital room that day, I was braced for the question I knew she would ask. Although she was happy, her face reflected a great deal of pain—this was her second caesarean operation. Braxton had been a placenta previa baby and had to be taken by caesarean, too. I almost lost both of them in that birth. So now as she lifted her head and cooed over Jacob, "Isn't he the most beautiful baby you have ever seen?" who in his right mind would argue with that?

I responded as I had with Braxton, and later would at the birth of our third son, Donny. "Yes, honey, he is the most beautiful baby I have ever seen."

Satisfied, she laid her head back on her pillow, closed her eyes, then quickly opened them again, looking at me squarely.

"You better be sure that's what you tell everyone else, too!"

Grinning, I bent down and gave her a kiss. She was still a little groggy from the surgery. Stroking her hair and rubbing her hands, I wanted this moment to last forever.

From the very first time that I saw Jacob, I knew in my heart that God had blessed us with another special son. Not long after he learned to walk he was trying to ride Braxton's bicycle. Jakie, as we affectionately called him, was just past two when we gave him a new blue (his favorite color) Schwin bike with training wheels. Was he proud! We had to put blocks on the pedals so his feet could reach.

Before long he begged to have the training wheels taken off.

"I'm old enough to ride by myself!"

"But Jakie . . . "

"I am! I know I can do it. Just give me a chance, please? Pleeeeease?"

We kept saying, "No, no, no . . . "

And he kept saying, "Yes, yes, yes . . . "

He insisted, "Just give me a try . . . okay?"

I said, "All right, I'll take them off, but if you can't ride the bike I'll have to put them right back on, understand?"

"I'll be able to ride it. I know I will."

Sure enough, after about three tumbles, and a few two-foot rides, he was off. Along a little hill by my dad's house Jacob had found a fence that started at the ground, and as the hill dropped down the fence got taller. He stepped onto the fence and from there onto the bike and pushed himself off, and away he went. No problems from then on.

Jacob at age 4

By the time he was three, he was riding a small Suzuki motorcycle by himself, and he was becoming proficient in baseball and soccer. At the age of four, he outplayed most children three and four years older than himself. He had exceptional coordination and balance, and he was determined to succeed at everything he tried.

Jacob seemed gifted with athletic ability. From the moment he awoke until the time he went to bed, he would have a ball in his hand. He bounced it off the floor, the walls, even the ceilings. One morning I was awakened by a pounding on the outside wall of our house. Curious, I pulled open the curtains and there was Jacob grinning at me as he threw the ball against the house one more time. That became a favorite early-morning activity of his.

When I was growing up, my father was a good baseball player. My brother and I always thought we had inherited some of his ability. We hoped that our kids would, too. I had always looked forward to doing with my boys what my dad had done with us. Jacob was like my baseball alter ego.

I noticed his talent in little things. My father had to drill my brother and me in how to catch a ball. With Jacob, this seemed to come naturally. He would position his body just right, and he knew just how to hold his glove regardless how high or low the ball flew.

I will always remember Jacob's first Little League game when he hit his first home run. He struck the pitch with a loud crack, sending the ball high over the second baseman's head. The cheers of the crowd quickly turned into frustrated yelling.

"The other way! The other way!" everyone screamed.

Oblivious to the crowd, he raced to third base, to second, to first, then sprinted across home plate. It didn't phase him a bit when he had to rerun the bases the right way.

The coach came up to me later, shaking his head. "That's the cockiest kid I've ever seen! But he's got a reason to be. I can't believe he's so good. Did you work with him a lot?"

"I'd like to take the credit, but I can't," I beamed.

One of Jacob's big thrills in life was to prove his ability. In December of 1982, a few weeks after his sixth birthday, he attended his first baseball camp. Two and three years younger than the other kids in the Bill Gray School of Baseball, he soon moved to the top of the class. On the field he would watch the other players and listen to the coach, then apply what he learned. When a ball sailed toward him, he was ready for it. He had what is called "soft hands." He didn't fight the ball, but brought it into him, setting himself into position to throw it. This technique was natural to Jacob.

Bill Gray, Sr., a Major League baseball scout for more than thirty years, loved the enthusiasm and confidence that Jacob had, and he laughed as Jakie would try to show the older boys what to do. On one occasion Mr. Gray turned on the "Jugs Machine" that shoots out fly balls, and the kids were to see how many they could catch in a row. The most anyone caught was ten in a row. Finally, it was Jacob's turn. He bent over as an outfielder would, with his hands resting on his knees, ready to go. The first ball shot out, Jacob moved underneath it, tapped his glove and caught it with two hands. Mr. Gray was impressed that he used two hands instead of trying to catch the ball with just one. Jacob caught thirty-three balls in a row, and fifty-one out of fifty-five. The other boys began to listen when Jacob talked.

Next was the hitting machine. Each boy started with the machine set at 35 miles per hour. All did fairly well until the speed was moved up to 45. This was getting pretty fast for the others, but Jacob hit ten of the twelve he received. By this time a group of parents had gathered around to watch. The bat was almost as big as Jacob was, but he knew just where to grip it for the hit. All the spectators were wondering about this little boy, when one of them finally asked the question I loved to hear.

"Whose kid is that?"

I felt this big grin crawl across my face, as if I were the one hitting the ball, and I said, "He's mine!"

The machine was turned up to 60 miles per hour. Jacob missed the first pitch, but automatically moved his hands up on the bat and hit line drives on eight of the next nine pitches.

From this baseball school, Jakie was invited by Mr. Gray to attend another school that he ran in Hemet, California, for boys ten to twelve years of age. Jakie was excited, and so were his mother and father. We could hardly wait to get home and call our families and friends.

Later we took Jacob and Braxton to the baseball camp in Hemet. When we arrived, a scout from the Boston Red Sox was signing the boys in. He took one look at Jacob and said, "Sorry, you're too small to be in this camp." Jakie gulped hard, tears welling in his eyes. He hated it when people told him he was too small or too young. He always thought he should be judged on his ability and nothing else. Just then Mr. Gray walked up.

"This is Jacob Gregg," he bragged to the scout. "You've got to see him."

Jacob flashed his usual grin when he realized he was going to be judged by his ability, not his size. He determined to prove to the scout that he deserved to be there.

At the end of the camp's nine weekends, Jacob left Hemet having proved to the scout that he did indeed belong there, and that he had a future in baseball . . .

I turned on my side to give Braxton and Donny more room in the bed. Exhausted, I tried to fall asleep. My thoughts, however, returned me to another side of Jacob.

Jacob was all boy, mischievous and full of pranks. One night as our family prepared to leave for Europe, Jacob, Braxton and I headed for the market which was just around the corner from our house. Jakie skipped ahead out of my sight and entered the parking lot. He made a gesture to a man driving out of the lot. The driver slammed on his brakes, jumped out of his car and was running toward Jacob just as Braxton and I rounded the corner.

"What are you doing!" I shouted at the man.

"That kid just flipped me off!" he fumed.

"I did not, Dad!" Jacob smirked. "I used *this* finger." He held up his ring finger. Turning to the obviously still angry man, he stuck out his chin and teased, "Fooled you!"

Jacob frequently visited our senior citizen neighbors, Eleanor and Esther. The moment they met, Eleanor thought Jacob was a little angel. The weather was cold, and he was sitting on a wooden stroller dressed in a leather jacket, his brown hair hanging a little below his ears.

"You have a scratch on your head," she smiled, introducing herself.

"My brudder doed it," he grinned proudly.

From then on, they were the best of friends. He would spend hours talking to Eleanor and Esther, charming them with his wit. On one occasion Eleanor picked up two bibs at a restaurant and handed them to Jacob.

"These will look terrific on Donny," she chuckled. "Just his size."

"I shall take just one," he said with a matter-of-fact tone. "You keep the other. You might marry again and have a baby just like me."

Once Jacob asked Eleanor if he could pick a few oranges for her. "Why yes, Jacob, you may," she patronized. "But I don't want you to become tired."

Squealing with delight, he grabbed a bucket which Eleanor offered and bounded for the orange tree. A few minutes later he returned with three spoiled oranges and asked for twenty-five cents.

"That's not worth twenty-five cents," she protested.

"Yes, but I'm t-i-r-e-d!" he grinned slyly.

He took special delight in teasing Braxton and getting him into trouble. In playing catch with the boys, I tried to teach them not to be afraid of a baseball. Like my father had done with my brother and me when we were first learning to catch, I would hit Jakie and Braxton with the ball — not hard — so they would realize it really didn't hurt that badly. As the boys played catch, Jacob would deliberately hit Braxton with the ball. When Braxton would get angry, Jakie would laugh, "I'm just teaching you not to be afraid of the ball!"

Jacob would often throw himself against the wall of his room, then scream, "Brackie hit me. He's beating me up." When Peggy or I would rush in to scold Braxton, Jacob would giggle. No matter how many times he tried this stunt, it would work.

On another occasion, I had leased a car and didn't have it a full day before noticing a ding on one side. Irritated, I

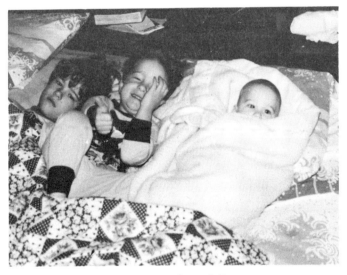

From left: Braxton, Jacob and Donny

stormed into the house and demanded, "Okay, who hit my car?"

Jacob faced me with a twinkle in his eye and pointed at his brother. "It was Brackie, Dad," he smiled mischievously.

"Did you hit the car, Braxton?" I asked calmly.

Braxton glared at Jacob. "I didn't hit it, Jakie. *You* threw the ball!"

"Maybe so. But you didn't catch it," Jacob grinned.

Jacob could hold grudges, too. When Donny was a newborn, Peggy was changing him on our bed. She didn't get the diaper on Donny quick enough and he wet all over. Jacob was hit with the spray. He became so angry that he later tried to wet on Donny.

On another occasion, Braxton hit Jacob. When he cried, Braxton jeered, "Cry baby, cry baby, cry baby!"

"I'll get you for that!" Jakie screamed.

"No you won't. You're too little!" Braxton taunted.

But get even Jacob did. While Braxton was asleep, he hit him with a plastic bat.

In the nearly seven years that God had granted Jacob to us, I never heard that boy say, "I can't." About three weeks before the accident, I took him to Magic Mountain, a popular Southern California amusement park. He had won the trip as a reward for memorizing Bible verses.

Children were measured at the gate to determine the appropriate admission charge. Because of his height, we had to pay the adult rate for him. At the roller coaster, he was measured again, this time to see if he was tall enough for the ride.

The monitor stood a measuring pole next to Jacob and shook his head. "Sorry, kid. You're too short."

"I'm gonna catch the biggest fish!" At age 6, Jacob went camping whenever he could.

"I caught the biggest!" A proud moment.

With tears streaming down his cheeks, he ran toward me. "Dad, they said I can't do it."

"Jacob, what do you think?"

"I can do it, Dad!" he brightened.

"How?"

He whispered in my ear, and I smiled in agreement. We sat down and took off Jacob's shoes. He peeled off his socks, and with them we built an additional two inches inside his shoes.

Jacob could hardly contain himself as he bounded toward the roller coaster. He rode it several times, grinning triumphantly each time he passed the guy who had told him he couldn't.

One of Jacob's favorite ways to tease a person was to call him a "dipstick." And if he knew it bothered him, he would rub it in. In my mind I could see Jacob in Heaven, going through a receiving line and being introduced to everyone, when he sees Saint Peter walking toward him. Holding onto Jesus' hand, he would look up into His eyes and ask, "Who's the dipstick?"

Lying in that dark room thinking about Jacob, I could not help smiling to myself. I would cherish these memories forever.

Jacob had lived and played like he enjoyed life and wasn't going to be cheated out of one moment of it. I tried not to think how life would have been for him had he survived the surgery and not been able to be so active, and I felt foolish for wanting to hold on to him.

The warm night had grown cool, and I pulled the blanket over my shoulder. Once again, fond remembrances crept across my mind.

Jacob at a karate picnic. He loved to wear a baseball uniform, and would wear it every day if you let him.

5

In Protective Hands

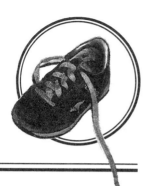

As committed as Jacob was to baseball, he was more devoted to the Lord. He couldn't get enough of God, the church, Royal Rangers—anything that had to do with the house of God. He wanted to be there every day.

He could not comprehend how people could live without going to church. On Saturdays he would call many of his friends, inviting them to church. Invariably their parents would say no, but he would call them back later to see if they had changed their minds.

Whenever possible, Braxton and Jacob enjoyed going with me to the church early in the mornings. One particular summer day stands out in my mind.

Not wishing to feel rushed, I rose early to take a leisurely shower while the rest of my family slept. I planned to arrive at the church early. Having promised the boys they could go with me this morning, I intended to awaken them at the appropriate moment. When I stepped into the living room, however, there they sat—

dressed in their corduroys and jeans and tennis shoes — beaming with excitement.

"Hurry up, Dad," Jacob piped. "It's gettin' late . . . "

They had everything all worked out. As soon as I was ready, we would all go out to breakfast. Then we would go to the church where they could throw the ball up against the building in the parking lot while I worked.

Obediently, I hurried through my shower, dressed faster than ever before, and re-entered the living room to announce that I was ready.

"What took you so long?" Jacob teased, as the boys bounded for the front door.

We laughed and talked between bites at a local cafe before heading for my office. They seemed unusually vibrant this morning, and I began to wonder what else they had in mind besides bouncing a ball off the church building all day. As we drove, I decided to find out.

Jacob and Braxton glanced at each other as if to say, "Don't you dare tell!" and giggled. "Don't worry, Dad," they laughed mischievously. "We've got the whole day figured out."

We arrived at the church by 8 o'clock. I headed for my office, and they bounded toward the youth hall. Assuming they were going to get a basketball or baseball and play catch in the parking lot, I buried myself in the day's tasks. However, when I didn't see or hear from them for two hours, I decided to investigate.

Finally, I found them. Jacob was standing on a chair in the sanctuary behind the pulpit, preaching his first message to his brother. Peering through the narrowly open door, I could hardly contain my laughter as he leaned over the pulpit to make a point. He stuck out his right index finger — just as he had seen his daddy do — and raised his little voice.

"Do you know Jesus?" he screeched.

"Amen!" Braxton yelled triumphantly.

That was all I could take. I threw the door open wide and began to applaud. "You're doing a great job, Jacob!" I complimented.

He gazed at me and, without skipping a beat, asked, "Do *you* know Jesus as your personal Savior? I don't mean do you know *about* Him. I want to know if you really *know* Him!"

Jacob spoke with such intensity that I realized he really meant business. Amazed, I slipped into one of the pews and listened. Quoting passages of Scripture that he had been memorizing since he was three, he spoke with conviction about his Friend, Jesus. When he was through, I realized just how much my little boy loved Jesus—and how much he knew Him. I was fascinated by the incredible simplicity of his message. What took Jacob fifteen minutes to deliver would have taken me forty-five, yet we would both come to the same conclusion. I usually spend a major portion of my time building an elaborate foundation, but he made his message so simple that anyone hearing him could understand.

The memory of this incident and the knowledge that he had such a grasp of what those Scriptures meant gave me great comfort as I lay in my bed the night of his death. My little boy didn't go to Heaven as a stranger—he was familiar with God's Word and God's people.

I thought how difficult we adults make salvation. We have to close our eyes, bow our head, and say this or that. Jacob's faith was simple.

He also had a way of testing me to see whether or not I believed what I preached. Having finished an extensive two-year Scripture memory course, he knew well what

God's Word says about the major truths of the gospel. One day he challenged me on healing.

Not feeling well, I came home early from church and flopped down on our bed. I had just gotten comfortable when Jacob strode in with his baseball glove and a ball.

"Dad. Let's play some catch."

"Not today, Jacob," I sighed. "I'm not feeling well."

Without a word, he reached down his hand and placed it on my head. "In the name of Jesus, be whole," he commanded. Then he smiled and threw his glove to me. "Let's play catch."

I hesitated and started to mumble something.

"Do you believe what you preach?" he interrupted.

"Yes, I do, Jacob," I groaned.

"Good! Let's play catch."

He had me. He asked, he believed, and now the question was whether or not I was going to receive. Challenged in faith by a six-year-old boy, I slipped my legs over the side of the bed and followed him outside. The funny thing about it was that I no longer felt sick!

Family has always been top priority with the Greggs. In decision making, for example, Peggy and I have involved the boys, explaining to them how our relationship with Christ influences our conclusions. Doing fun things together is high on our list. Spiritual matters, however, come first. Peggy and I frequently read Bible stories and discuss them with our children. Often our discussions center on what makes a person special to God, and what it means to give oneself completely to the Lord.

Jacob took this counsel seriously and applied it to everything he did. In Royal Rangers, our denomination's scouting program for young boys, his rapid advancement reflected a zeal that spoke of his devotion to God as well as his competitive drive.

He was a Straight Arrow Brave, a Straight Arrow Tribesman and a Straight Arrow Warrior. These names seemed appropriate for him, for when he spoke to you, it was straight from his heart. Many times I shared with Jakie and Braxton the humorous and serious sides of my ministry, encouraging them to ask questions about things they didn't understand. I talked to them about the excitement of seeing someone come to the Lord. Often when Jacob and I were together, we spoke of what a privilege it is to be part of God's kingdom.

Peggy and I were competitive in cultivating the love of our children. In the process, we would ask the boys (in fun, of course), "Who do you love the best?" meaning Peggy or me. Because we instilled in them that they belong to the Lord and are just in our care, their response was always *Jesus*.

Sunday, August 28, the last time we saw Jacob alive, was so much like any other day in his life. He spent the morning and evening at God's house and the afternoon at home playing with his brothers. Later in the afternoon — his favorite time — he played catch with his daddy.

As church ended that night, Peggy and I loaded the boys into the car for the trip to San Diego. Braxton and Jacob were to spend a week with my parents before starting back to school.

Everything was exciting to the boys. They chattered about the things they were going to do, and Jacob smiled mischievously as he thought of the tricks he would play on his Papaw.

As we drove to San Diego, everyone became hungry at the same time, and we stopped at a Carl's Jr. Gathered around the table, we bantered and laughed as we had done

Jacob told his daddy, "I know Donny thinks there's a Santa, but I'm not going to spoil it for him."

many times before. It didn't occur to us that this time could be any different. Soon we finished and were on the road again. Peggy, Braxton, and Donny fell asleep, leaving Jacob and me to watch the road and talk. We chatted for awhile about baseball, then he leaned back in the seat and looked at me thoughtfully.

"Daddy, there's no such thing as Santa Claus," he blurted, his face knitted into a slight frown. "I know that, but Donny thinks there is. Dad, I'm not going to spoil it for him."

I gazed at him for a moment, then smiled. "Jacob, you're a good brother," I complimented.

We arrived at my folks house at approximately 11:30 P.M. Since I had appointments early the next morning, Peggy and I had decided not to stay. We tucked Braxton and Jacob into bed and kissed them good night. Saying goodbye to my parents, we scooped a sleepy Donny into our arms and headed for home.

All the way, Peggy and I thanked God for blessing us with our boys, and we spoke of their love for each other. I mentioned what Jacob had said about Santa Claus, and Peggy shared something that she heard him say to Donny just a few days earlier.

Standing with his arm around his little brother, talking to him as he so frequently did, Jacob had said, "Donny, if you ever say a bad word, you don't have to close your eyes, just say, 'Jesus forgive me,' and He will."

That was Jacob, so simple and so direct.

As I lay in the bed, fighting the stinging tears of the memory, my mind raced ahead to what could have been. I felt robbed—robbed of his company, his love, his life.

Suddenly my tears erupted into uncontrollable sobs. I eased out of bed and crawled underneath it to be alone in my sorrow. With my body heaving under the sobs, I began to feel a familiar presence.

"Whatcha doin', Dad?"

Words can hardly describe what I heard and saw. Barefoot and dressed in his shorts and baseball shirt, his hands stuffed in his pockets, Jacob stooped low to grin mischievously at me under the bed.

He had asked me that question many times during his short life. Often when I took my church work home, thinking that the world would go to Hell if I didn't finish what I was doing, he would help me bring things into perspective with his impish smile and "Whatcha doin', Dad?"

"I'm crying," I sniffled, startled.

"Why?"

"I'm crying because I hurt, Jacob."

He crawled under the bed with me, and I was mesmerized by the sight of his joyful face. Only hours before I had seen his pale form lying cold and still, his head tucked into a white skull cap, his face bruised and swollen. In this precious moment, however, he was the little boy that I knew, put back together again.

"Daddy, aren't I where you always wanted me to be?"

With those words, he smiled and vanished. How can I describe this experience? Was it a dream, a vision? I don't know, but his appearance and our conversation were real to me.

A moment before, I had been the loneliest man in the world, abandoned to my sorrow—very much like David when he cried over his slain son, "Absalom, Absalom, my son, Absalom!" Now an indescribable peace crept over me. My heavenly Father had known where I was and had sent my boy to me. I stayed under the bed for a few more minutes enjoying His comfort and pondering what Jacob had said. When God had blessed Peggy and me with each of our children, we had prayed that they would one day go to Heaven.

Wiping my eyes, I smiled slightly. "Yes, you are where we always wanted you to be, Jacob. You're in the tender care of Jesus."

With a clearer perspective on our loss, I edged out from my hiding place and climbed back into bed. The assurance that we all were in God's protective hands brought me quick sleep.

6

Unseen Forces

A short time later I awoke to the sound of voices. Peggy and the boys were still asleep but other members of our family were stirring.

The words of a familiar song began to filter through my mind:

> Tell it to Jesus, tell it to Jesus,
> He is a friend who's well known.
> There's no other such a friend or brother,
> Tell it to Jesus alone.

Quietly, I slipped out of bed and knelt.

Though comforted by my experience with Jacob, my confidence in God's protective hands was still shaky. Growing up in a Christian home, I had often heard people talk about such things as miracles and guardian angels. I was skeptical about God's protection, however, because I had suffered so many things both as a child and as an adult. I didn't feel protected, and I wasn't sure that I could accept Jacob's death as one of those "all things work together for good" experiences.

65

"Lord, I'm not one of Your spiritual giants," I whispered. "I'm just an ordinary person who happens to be a pastor. I have a heart for You, and I want to serve You, but I can't trust my life and my family to someone who's not able to do what he says he can do. I must know in my heart that You are in complete control. If I'm going to make it through this, I need to see Your hand in Jacob's death. I need to see the little things around me that will show me You are with us."

This was perhaps the first time that I was openly honest with God, not trying to phrase my prayer in just the right way to impress Him. I had thought my prayers were from the heart, but now it was different. I could not formulate "proper" words; my heart was too broken. What He heard was what I really was—defenseless and fearful.

I had accepted Jacob's death yesterday. I had received comfort last night. This, however, was a new day. Faced with making funeral arrangements today, I felt the reality that my little boy was gone hitting me with renewed force.

Peggy and the boys began to stir. I rose slowly from my knees and quickly dressed.

Peggy _____

My first thought when I awakened was that I had been having a nightmare—my usual experience when I'm seriously ill. The night before the accident, I had begun to have great difficulty breathing. Gasping and feeling pressure in my chest, I had gotten up in the wee hours of the morning and was running around the house in a panic. Don beat me on the back until I could breathe again. Last night I had a hard time breathing as well. This morning the sound of voices outside our room startled and angered me. My world had stopped, and I couldn't imagine how anyone else's could still be going on.

Slipping on my robe, I stepped into the living room to join the others, but not feeling a part of their world, I decided to call a friend of mine. She was down to earth, and I needed someone like her to help pull things together for me.

Using the phone in a back bedroom, I dialed slowly. "Hello, Esther? Jacob didn't make it," I began. "He died."

"I know," she responded calmly.

"Well, I don't know what to do."

Esther was quiet, not knowing how to answer me.

"I feel lost and I feel scared and I really don't know what to do right now," I whimpered.

Still no response.

"Well, I just called to see if you knew what I was supposed to do now," I continued.

"I'm really sorry, Peggy . . . "

Marcie Collingwood, a close friend of David and Gracia's, was in the living room when I rejoined the family. She had lost her husband and son two years before, and had given David and Gracia her son's bicycle, the one Jacob had been riding. We embraced when I entered the room, then sat together in silence while all the others visited. The kinship I felt in her silence was comforting. No words could express the feelings we shared.

Don and I had attended her husband and son's funeral. I could still picture her shaking hands and greeting all those who attended the service. Then, as now, I couldn't handle the seemingly mundane conversations that surrounded her.

Soon, Peggy, I said to myself, *you'll be in her place. You're going to be the one greeting the people.*

The thought haunted me.

Finally, Dad and Mom took everyone out to breakfast. I stayed behind to make the arrangements for Jacob's body to be transferred to Los Angeles for the funeral, and to spend more time alone with God.

Between phone calls, I felt the Lord speak to my heart about the prophet Elisha and his servant when they were surrounded by the enemy. I picked up a Bible and turned to the story recorded in 2 Kings 6:8-17 to refresh my memory.

The king of Syria was warring against Israel. Each time Syria mobilized its forces to attack, the prophet would warn Israel and reveal the location of Syria's troops. This happened several times before the king of Syria realized what Elisha was doing. Learning that the prophet was in Dothan, the king dispatched his army to seize him. The Syrian forces surrounded the city during the night. When Elisha's servant awoke early the next morning and went outside, he was panic stricken. Enemy troops, horses and chariots were everywhere.

"What are we going to do?" the servant cried out to Elisha.

"Don't be afraid," the prophet calmed. "Our army is bigger than theirs!"

Then Elisha asked the Lord to open the young man's eyes. The unseen forces of God — a cavalry of angelic warriors with their fiery horses and chariots — had encircled the enemy.

Reading that portion of Scripture in the past, my mind had focused on Elisha. To me the servant was just a two-bit player in the story of a prophet's great faith. As I read that passage today, however, I felt electrified. I was that servant, and God was speaking to me, "Open your eyes, Don, to the unseen forces around you. I'm going to let you see what I see."

I was one of those guys who believed that if you can't see something, it must not be real. The unspiritual man tends to discount that which he cannot see or measure. He wrongly concludes that his five senses take in everything. He takes stock of men, money and materials, concluding that there is nothing else in life. I determined not to fall into that category. I needed something to believe in. I needed to know that we weren't facing this crisis by ourselves, that God was in control. I reflected on an immense truth recorded in the Book of Hebrews: "Faith . . . is the conviction of things not seen" (Hebrews 11:1 NASB). It is the ability to know and believe in that which goes beyond our five senses. Closing the Bible, I prayed, "Lord, I trust You to show me the things that are not seen. Let my eyes be open and let me see that the armies of God are really on my side."

My first glimpse of His unseen forces came when I called the Turner and Stevens Mortuary in Alhambra to arrange Jacob's funeral. Having conducted many services there as a pastor, I was well acquainted with the manager, Chuck Hayden.

"I have a favor to ask," I began after Chuck came to the phone.

"Sure, what can I do for you?"

"Yesterday, my little boy . . . Jacob . . . was hit by a car and killed. I need someone to take care of him as if he were his own. His body is at the coroner's office for an autopsy, and I need to get him back up to L.A. I don't know what to do . . . " my voice cracked.

"Don't worry about a thing, Don. I'll take care of everything." The concern in his voice was comforting. I sensed that he felt the loss of Jacob keenly, even though he had never met him.

"What about the casket?" I wondered. "I've never been to a child's funeral. Do you use a small casket or a regular sized one?"

"We'll have to order one special," he informed. "You'll need to pick out what you want so we can get the order in right away. I'll go to the factory with the order myself. When are you coming home?"

"We'll be there tonight. I have to go to the coroner's office this afternoon and sign some papers."

"With the Labor Day weekend coming up, we're racing against time. You'll need to be in my office by nine o'clock tomorrow morning to go over the arrangements." He asked me to request Jacob's measurements from the coroner and bring them with me.

"Are we going to be able to handle all this so quickly?" I asked. "If you have other commitments, I'll understand . . ."

"Don't worry about it, Don. We're family. We're in this together."

Because Chuck is involved with death all the time, he could have been cold and calloused. However, when he said "family," I knew that God had begun to show me His hand. I had always taught my boys that there is nothing more important than the family. I wanted each of the boys to know that his relationship with God was first, but family was next. You can have friends, but never think that your friends are going to be better to you than your family. Chuck was an outsider, but he couldn't have said anything more comforting. This was a word that God knew I desperately needed to hear. From that moment, a member of my family would be taking care of Jacob.

The enemy doesn't strike us where we're strong. He attacks us in our vulnerable areas. As the day wore on, Satan bombarded my mind with doubts and fears—and a sense of smallness that was foreign to me. I was used to controlling my situations. Usually, I could walk into a room and be the most dominant person there without having to say a word. I prided myself in providing for my family.

Now, one of them was gone, and I felt helpless. Even with the forces of God surrounding me, I could still see the Syrian army in my circumstance. The awesomeness of making arrangements to bury my son was overwhelming. I was going to put him in a box and bury him in the ground.

Is there really a resurrection? I wondered. *Suppose the grave doesn't open up? Suppose there is no Heaven? Will I ever see that boy again?* I had gone through many years of schooling and pastoring, saying—hopefully—the right things to people in their times of grief. I never believed that such thoughts would cross my mind, but here they were, one after the other, haunting, badgering until it seemed that the forces of Syria were pressing around me and gaining strength; death was winning, and my faith was beginning to crumble.

Sitting beside the phone, my thoughts turned toward the coming Sunday. I sensed God leading me to share the things that I would learn in the next three days, but how could I preach so soon? The realization that I had to face my congregation on Sunday introduced another pressure. How I handled the loss of my son would be vital to their lives. What could I say to them?

"Lord," I protested, "it's not fair! Jacob just died, and You're telling me to preach on Sunday? Can't I have a few days to myself?"

His answer flashed through my mind so unmistakably that the words couldn't have been more clear had they been audible. "No. You need to put into practice what you've so often preached."

"I know the right things to say, Lord," I objected, "but I'm not sure I can tell the people that I buy them."

"Why?" the question came.

"I'm just not sure anymore. I'm still trying to sort things out. I can't stand in that pulpit and tell those people how great You are if I don't feel it. I need time."

"Why do you need more time?"

"I'm saying the right things to You now, Lord, but that's today. This is just a day after the accident. I'm not ready. This is a brand new step for me."

"Remember Peter in the boat? He walked on the water. When my Son said 'Come,' that was a big step, too. Are you going to trust Me? It is not important how you feel right now. It is what I say through you that counts. Your people will understand that you are not an authority on death, but you must put into practice what you have preached. They must see the shoe leather on the ground now."

"But, Lord, what am I going to share with them?" I persisted.

"The truth. Tell them you are a struggler, like Elisha's servant. Tell them that it is by My grace and strength that you will get through your sorrow. They need to know also that they can't make it by themselves, that they can open their eyes and see that I am there because the angel of the Lord encampeth round about those who fear Him."

Except for these moments in prayer and in meditation upon God's Word, I spent most of the morning on the telephone. It wasn't too far into the day that calls began to come from all over the country to express condolences and pray for our family.

By late morning the family had not yet returned from breakfast. Since my calls were completed, I decided to go for a walk and ponder what the Lord had been saying to me. I stepped outside and noticed a familiar pickup parked across the street. *That must be Roger,* I mused. *Wonder why he doesn't come in?*

When I approached, tears were in Roger's eyes. "I just don't understand it, Don," he sniffled. "Everything seems to happen to you. I just can't believe it . . . "

I stepped around to the other side of the pickup and slipped into the passenger seat. Roger, my cousin, had seen me through all the bad times when I wasn't serving the Lord and knew how easy it would have been for me cry the blues. Because I had a willing ear and because someone who loved me thought I was getting a raw deal, the temptation to wallow in self-pity was strong. At this moment the unseen forces were again swinging their swords. Would the army of Syria overwhelm me, or would the warriors of Heaven be victorious? Would I trust God, or succumb to self-pity? The choice was mine.

Roger and I cried and laughed together for nearly an hour about Jacob and incidents in our own lives. In our precious moments together he observed—and I experienced—an inner strength that I had never known before. We began to understand the difference between self-pity and grieving. It's all right to cry when you're hurting. Jesus wept over the loss of Lazarus even though He was about to raise him from the dead. Self-pity is self-centered and destructive. While grief is personal, it can be constructive when it focuses on the positives remaining in our lives.

"I couldn't control what happened," I told Roger. "I've got to hope that God is going to bring something good out of it. His Word promises that 'all things work together for good.' I still have two wonderful boys and a lovely wife who took such great care of Jacob. I couldn't ask for anything more."

My great need in these early stages of grief was a sense of family. The bonding that took place between Roger and me went far beyond our common name. Our kinship had become one of the heart. So it was earlier that morning between me and another cousin, Larry. He had learned of Jacob's death while at work and had rushed over. I had not seen him in nearly two years. He threw his arms around my shoulders and greeted me with tears.

In my fellowship with Larry and Roger, I began to see God's hand in healing our family. I sensed He would repair other bonds in the days to come.

The family returned while Roger and I talked. Another cousin, Charlie, also had arrived. As he and David approached, I glanced at my watch. It was past noon. We all exchanged pleasantries for a moment, then I asked them to accompany me to the coroner's office in Mira Mesa, a suburb of San Diego. Some papers had to be signed and other arrangements made so the mortuary could pick up Jacob's body. I wasn't prepared for that encounter.

Introducing myself to a coroner's assistant, I asked to see Jacob.

"Sir, I don't think that would be a good idea," he objected. "It's not like a hospital here; it's very plain and stark, and . . . "

"Look, I'm the boy's father!" I interrupted. "I want to see my son!"

Stunned by my tone, the assistant tried to explain. "He won't look anything like you expect him to look . . . "

"It won't matter; I need to see him," I insisted.

He stepped to a back room and soon emerged with the coroner. As politely as possible, he too attempted to discourage me, explaining that he could not cover the scars on Jacob's body from the transplant operation nor from the autopsy.

"I still want to see my son. I need to measure him, and I need to know his weight!" My persistence obviously was making everyone uneasy.

"I'm sorry, Mr. Gregg, I don't think that would be advisable. I don't think you can handle it." The firmness of the coroner's voice told me it was useless to argue.

"Okay," I sighed, admitting finally that he was right.

After the coroner provided me with the information I needed, and all the necessary papers were signed, we left. I felt embarrassed over my actions. The coroner had treated me professionally and courteously, despite my impatience. I had expected the warmth of Chuck Hayden and was stunned by their seemingly cold refusal. Perhaps God was showing me both sides—the warmth of family and the coldness of professionalism—so that I would realize the depth of His care in the coming days.

By the time we returned to my parents' home, friends and relatives had begun to arrive. How easy it would be for emotions to get out of control and hurtful words to be spoken. The ramifications of a child dying while in the care of relatives and how we would respond was a heavy burden. I wondered what they were expecting. Hurting as I was, I would have to be strong for the sake of others. I would have to put on a happy face, smiling as though everything was all right, realizing that I wasn't able to grieve openly. Not yet. My time would come later.

The greatest pressure we faced was dealing with the feelings of vulnerability and the sense of responsibility which several of our family felt for the accident, and how it would affect our relationships—Gracia, because our boys were under her care; David, because he had let them ride the bikes; Dad, because we had placed them in his care and he had let them go over to David and Gracia's; and Mom, simply because she is my mom. We weren't angry at any of them, but it seemed that the room was full of eyes, each watching us intently to detect the slightest hint of resentment or to judge how we were responding to our loss. Lovingly, we sought to reassure the family that we didn't hold them responsible for Jacob's death.

From the start, I felt cheated that I couldn't just be a father in this situation. It seemed unfair that Peggy and I had to be so concerned about everybody else's needs. I wanted to be alone with Peggy and to collect my thoughts. No one seemed to be aware of that; they all needed to feel our acceptance.

About 7 o'clock we prepared to leave for home. Drained and exhausted, we said our goodbyes and began the long journey toward Los Angeles. The phone rang shortly after we arrived. It was a fellow minister whom I had wronged a few years before. We had talked since that time, but our conversations were always casual. Now he and his wife wanted to come over and minister healing to our broken hearts. Again, God was showing me that His unseen forces were still at work. He was restoring a relationship that I had injured.

Despite the lateness of the hour, we welcomed them. They embraced and loved us, praying that in the darkness of this night we would be able to see the light of morning.

7

Blooming in Another Garden

Tears were trickling down Chuck Hayden's face when he met us in his office at the mortuary early on Friday.

"Don, Peggy, I love you," he sniffled, throwing his arms around us in a firm hug. "I've been praying for you. Don't worry about a thing, I'm taking care of everything personally." Chuck motioned for us to be seated as we began to discuss Jacob's funeral arrangements.

Peggy and I were unaware of all the things that needed to be done at a time like this. How often I had been with others as they made arrangements for their departed loved ones, but had never stopped to evaluate what took place! Common sense, I assumed, was all that one needed. Little did I realize how little common sense one possesses in these moments.

Besides information about Jacob's birth, death, family and date and place of funeral, such things as a casket, burial plot and the type of clothing he would wear became major concerns for us. We wanted everything to be special, yet we weren't sure what would be best. We didn't want to skimp on the casket, but how much money should we spend? We needed help. Chuck began to advise us on the necessary decisions.

"How much money do you need for this," I sighed after signing some papers.

"Don't worry about money, we're not concerned about it now," Chuck assured.

His tears and loving hugs brought peace into our broken hearts. The knowledge that Jacob was being taken care of, not by a corporation merely concerned for money, but by extended members of our family who would handle him in the tenderest way, brought us great comfort as we returned to our car.

Chuck was true to his word. After we left, he ordered work to be started on the casket, then drove to San Diego to collect Jacob's body and death certificate. Later he personally picked up the casket from the manufacturer, and then began preparations for Jacob's viewing.

Meanwhile, we headed for the cemetery to view the lot that a member of our church had graciously given us. The night before, after we returned from San Diego, Pat Werner had called.

"I'm so sorry to hear about Jacob," she said solemnly. "You're going to need a place to bury him, and I want to give you my burial spot at Rose Hills."

"Thank you, Pat, but that won't be necessary . . . " I protested kindly.

"You must take it, Pastor," she insisted. "The Lord wants me to give it to you."

It's hard to say no to someone who has just told you that, so I accepted the plot.

Now as Peggy and I headed for the cemetery, I began to wonder about its location and all the silly things that I had laughed about for years. Was the gravesite on a hill? Did it have a good view? Was it shaded? Were there trees around? If so, what kind of roots did they have? Did the site have good drainage?

Those questions became very important as we sped along the freeway. I didn't want to make a mistake in accepting Pat's plot; at the same time, I surely didn't want to hurt her feelings.

Rose Hills is set on the sloping hills of Whittier. At the administration building we learned the location of the gravesite and followed instructions up the hill to a section called Suncrest. To my amazement, the burial plot was perfect. Set on a hill with a great view of Los Angeles, it was a serene and shaded place where we could visit and meditate about Jacob and the future.

My eye caught the grave marker next to Jacob's plot. Tears formed as I began to understand the magnitude of Pat Werner's gift. Jacob would lie next to her husband Don, who had died a few years earlier. We were overwhelmed with the love she had shown in giving us this very special place. Peggy and I marveled at God's loving care in every detail of our lives. Clearly His unseen forces were still at work.

Our next stop was Rossi's Flowers in Alhambra. Mr. Rossi was about to leave when we arrived. Although he had provided flowers free of charge to our church for many years, my only contact with him had been to say hello and thank him for his contributions.

We explained all that had happened and asked him to handle the flowers for Jacob. Mr. Rossi assured us that he would take personal charge of all floral provisions for the mortuary and the funeral. As we turned to leave, he handed Peggy a single red rose. That rose took on special significance in the days that followed. Placed in a small vase, it slowly unfolded, symbolizing to us the blossoming of Jacob's life even in death.

Peggy _____

Our next stop was the most difficult of all. It was mid-afternoon and we still had not bought Jacob's burial clothes. Neither of us could speak as we threaded our way through aisles of shoppers to the little boys' section of the huge department store.

Memories of other times we had rummaged through the clothing racks and tables for just the right shirt and pants for Jacob brought stinging tears. Finally, we could do no more than stand and weep.

"May I help you? What are you looking for?" a young voice behind us offered.

Don bit hard on his lip as we glanced at each other. "Yes. We're looking for something for our little boy to wear. He died, and we need something to bury him in."

Without a word, the young clerk turned slowly and retreated to wait on another customer.

I felt helpless and alone, barely able to think. *What should Jacob wear? What would look like him? Should we bury him in a baseball uniform, or in his church clothes?* All I could see were the shirts that he didn't like and I had always wanted him to wear. I could still hear him objecting, "I don't like that, Mom, I don't like that!"

"Honey, do you think he should wear this?" Don's question startled me. I shook my head.

None of the other clerks offered their help as we continued our search. To me, as long as we couldn't find what we wanted, we didn't have to bury Jacob. We finally settled on a pair of Levis, a plaid shirt, a blue sweater and blue socks. We bought the sweater because it seemed heartless to put him in the ground with just a shirt.

The cashier was solemn as she checked our items. *Did the clerk tell her about us?* I wanted to ask the cashier whether she thought our selections were appropriate but decided not to.

We decided that Jacob would wear the new shoes I bought him just before our trip to San Diego. He had done something that earned him a treat, and he wanted a pair of tiger-tooth slip-on tennis shoes. Don had objected, "You're not going to have little black and white diamonds all over your shoes."

But Jacob was always clever about figuring out the angles. When we returned with the shoes, he sidled up to Don and grinned impishly. "Dad, look at this."

"Jacob! I told you you couldn't get them!" Don exclaimed.

"You said black and white diamonds. These are black and white boxes," his grin broadened.

Don peered at the shoes, then shrugged. "I guess you're right!" Jacob had outsmarted him again.

He begged to take his new shoes with him to San Diego, but I refused. "Those are your school shoes," I explained. "You can't wear them until school starts."

Because he loved them so, we wanted him to wear them now.

We drove home to collect some other things of Jacob's before returning to the mortuary. Wondering whether he would need his underwear and belt, we packed them in a brown paper bag with the shoes and new clothes—just in case.

"He won't need the shoes," Chuck observed when we delivered the clothing.

"But we want Jacob in shoes," Don protested, aware this was not customary.

"It won't make any difference," Chuck shrugged. "People won't see them."

"That's all right. We still want him to wear his shoes," Don pressed.

Patiently, Chuck agreed. I was glad that Don insisted — on the day of the viewing, Donny lifted the bottom lid of the casket to see whether Jacob was wearing his shoes.

Don _____

Shortly after returning from the mortuary, I received a call from one of my church board members, Len Griswold.

"Phyllis and I want to take you out for coffee," he suggested. "We have something to share with you."

"Okay," I agreed, determined to say as little as possible.

At the appointed time, they arrived and we drove the few blocks to the restaurant. Peggy stayed home with guests who had begun to gather.

Our conversation was strained with each of us being careful what we said. Trying to be sensitive to how I was feeling, they attempted to minister to me.

"We were able to get in touch with our son," Phyllis said. Kevin, who had been working in Tokyo with Youth With a Mission for the past six months, was special to Jacob. I remembered with a smile the time he had taken Jacob out with the older kids one night after church. As

Phyllis spoke, I could still see the smile on Jacob's face as he strutted through the front door of our home after the outing, with Kevin following close behind.

"Did you have a good time?" I had asked.

"I sure did!" he beamed. Kevin even let me ride in the trunk on the way home!"

When Kevin heard of Jacob's death, Phyllis said, he was in the airport in Tokyo. "When he left the phone, he began to cry, 'Why, God? Why did You cut him down?' "

As Phyllis related this, I perked up. That was the question I wanted to ask, but was afraid to. Now, I was going to get the answer.

"God spoke to Kevin," Phyllis continued. "He said, 'Kevin, I didn't cut Jacob down like you think. I just reached under the soil and took him by the roots and planted him in another garden so he could blossom.' "

Later that evening I shared our conversation with Peggy. Those words of promise comforted our hearts and we determined not to let Jacob's death be a tragedy. We realized that if we allowed people to dwell on the loss of his life, they would lose sight of God's power and ability to perform miracles of salvation, healing and hope. Instead, we would ask them to look at his gain and the legacy that would be left in his memory.

In addition to the swirl of activity surrounding Jacob's death, we were in the process of moving. We had to be out of our house on Saturday. Peggy was suffering incredibly under the strain and, because of her physical condition, she was getting little sleep. Saturday morning she called Kathy, a close friend who lived in Apple Valley, some distance away, for help. Kathy arrived that evening. During the next few days she acted as a buffer for Peggy, shielding her from much of the pressure surrounding our family and freeing me to attend to the many things that had to be done.

A number of things needed to be done on our new house before we could move in, and a group from the church busied themselves all day getting it ready. Then the church moved us while we were having dinner with Peggy's parents.

Late that night, after everyone had gone to bed, I slipped into the dining room and sat at the table to gather my thoughts for Sunday's sermon. This was the first time since my few moments of prayer and meditation on Thursday morning that I had been able to concentrate on Sunday. I knew the gist of my message. God had given me the story of Elisha and his servant, but what was I going to say? Wearily, I jotted down a few handwritten notes and went to bed.

8

Peace Like a River

The next morning I stopped by the mortuary on my way to church to deliver some of Jacob's things. That afternoon, Jacob's body would be ready for viewing, and I wanted to make sure everything was all right.

My uncle had died suddenly of a heart attack while I was in high school, and I vividly recalled my father's trauma the first time he visited the mortuary. His brother's body had been poorly prepared, and it was barely recognizable because of extensive swelling. When we expressed our concerns to the attendants, they jerked the pillow from underneath his head and began to pound and push on his face in an attempt to reshape it, while we watched in horror. I wanted no surprises for my family this afternoon. I had to make sure Jacob looked natural.

Chuck Hayden greeted me with a hug when I arrived. "I want you to meet my assistant, Bill Sharrad," he said warmly.

"I'm so sorry about your son," Bill comforted, wrapping his arm around my shoulders. "I've been praying for you and your family. Chuck and I want you to know that we're your friends and want to do everything we can to lighten your load."

I nodded a thank you and asked to see Jacob.

"We put him in a double room," Chuck explained as he led us toward a door. "We thought maybe you would need both areas rather than the standard room."

The rooms were separated by double doors to provide privacy around the casket in one, while people met and talked in the other during the viewing.

I was amazed as we entered the rooms. Jacob's casket was already surrounded with flowers.

"How does he look?" Chuck wondered.

I gazed at Jacob for a moment, then nodded my approval. They had covered his bruises well. Our family would not have to worry about people's responses as they viewed his body.

"May I spend a few minutes alone with him?" My voice quivered.

As Chuck and Bill stepped quietly out of the room, I gingerly inserted Jacob's little black Royal Ranger New Testament between his folded hands and fastened his Sunday school award pins to his sweater.

I stood for a moment gazing through blurring eyes at his still form. "Jakie, I'm sorry if I ever let you down," I sobbed. "Your daddy's not perfect . . . but he always tried to do . . . what was right. You probably know more now about . . . just how imperfect your daddy is . . . but I want you to know that I always loved you."

I bent down and kissed him on the cheek and slowly turned away.

Sunday school had begun and the lot was empty of people when I drove into my parking space at the church.

Not wanting to see anyone as I went inside, I slipped into my office through the back entrance. Alone at my desk, I began to think of the people who would be in the service and what I would say to them.

"Lord, help me," I prayed, burying my head in my hands. "Lead me and guide me. You know the needs of these people far more than I do. You know what I need to say to them. I don't want the people to feel sorry for Peggy and me. Above all, I don't want them to think Jacob's death is a tragedy. Peggy and I want You to be glorified in this situation. Help us, Lord, to model how Christians should look to You in their grief and not blame You for what happens. God, help me to be transparent. May what I say this morning comfort other families who are struggling, and bring those who don't know Christ into a personal relationship with Him."

The morning worship was about to start when three of my staff members entered. We went over the order of service and determined that I should not appear until after the congregation was informed of Jacob's death.

When they left to begin the service, I shut off the lights in my office and inserted a cassette tape into my stereo. The familiar strains of "In My Life Be Glorified," Jacob's favorite song, filled the room.

Peggy _____

Dominic Palermo, the usher who usually escorted me to my seat on Sunday mornings, met us as we stepped into the foyer of the church. With me were Don's father and mother, his sister, David and Gracia, my father, mother and sister, Kathy and Betty and the children.

You have to know Dominic. He's excitable and hyper. "Okay, okay, everybody, just stand right here now!" he said loudly. "They haven't made the announcement yet."

Other late comers passed us, smiling and greeting me with their customary "hi." Realizing they still didn't know, I returned their smiles.

"Are you going to go down front with me like you always do?" Dominic asked nervously.

"Yes," I assured, wondering why we were not allowed to go into the service.

Finally the announcement was made, and I could hear the congregation gasp with unbelief. Jacob—who was so full of life, so mischievous, so loving—was a favorite to many. Some began to weep as a cloud of sadness settled over the auditorium. Tom Benton canceled the church picnic that had been scheduled for the afternoon and announced the viewing times at the mortuary. A special love offering was received on our behalf.

As the congregation began to lift the strains of the familiar hymn, *It Is Well With My Soul,* Dominic opened the door into the sanctuary. He took my arm and escorted me down the aisle to the third row from the front. The rest of the family followed close behind. Don entered the platform through a side door.

> When peace, like a river,
>   attendeth my way,
> When sorrows like sea billows roll;
> Whatever my lot,
>   Thou hast taught me to say,
> It is well, it is well with my soul.

Those words held special meaning for me as I listened. Philip Bliss had penned them after his wife and children perished at sea when their ship capsized and sank. Enveloped in a sense of peace and security, I felt privileged that God had now entrusted me with something sweet.

Don stepped to the pulpit and began to speak. I felt proud of him as he shared from his heart. The people were seeing their shepherd vulnerable, hurting, broken and transparent. All were painfully aware that losing a loved one was inevitable. Perhaps theirs would be a mother, a brother, an aunt or grandmother. Now they were gaining courage and hope for when they too would suffer loss. Their shepherd would not abandon them. He would understand their pain.

Don

I gripped the sides of the pulpit firmly as I looked out across the congregation and began to speak. "I want you to know, this is a very difficult time for me. Every Sunday I stand in this pulpit and tell you how to live . . . "

I paused for a moment to compose myself, then continued. "It would have been very easy for me to stay home today, to be locked up in my own grief. I was asked to take the day off, but you are very much a part of our family, and the hurt that we have felt has been shared by you. I would be less than your pastor if I weren't able to stand before you and tell you that we have found great solace in our hearts, and that the undergirding power of the Holy Spirit is real. In moments when Peggy and I thought we were alone, our elder Brother, Jesus, was there. He surrounded us with other members of our family who spoke to our hearts.

"Peggy and I are not in the service for you to feel sorry for us; we are here for you to rejoice with us that God allowed us the privilege of having that little boy."

I went on to tell the congregation how much joy Jacob had brought into our lives and how, though it was hard, we had given him back to God. I assured them, "We have no regrets, no changes to make. Jacob was not a stranger to the Lord Jesus. We know in our hearts that when our son was making his way across that 'valley of the shadow of death,' he was walking toward Someone he knew, and knew very well—Jesus Christ. This," I said, "is a great comfort to us."

As I spoke, the Holy Spirit poured strength into my spirit, strength to realize that the church family needed to see that God was big enough to meet our need so that they could trust Him to meet theirs.

This proved to be true in the months that followed. As members of our congregation lost loved ones, what they saw in us enabled them to trust God in their grief. In fact, one man told me flat out, "When God took Jacob, I didn't know if I could ever trust Him again. I didn't know If I wanted to serve Him or if I wanted to have someone like Him over my life, someone who would take a child so gifted as that boy. When I look around and see all the others He could have taken who didn't look like they had much of a future, and then realize He took Jacob, it didn't make sense to me.

"I needed to see you in the pulpit that Sunday morning because I needed to know how you felt."

I shared what the Lord had revealed to me the morning after Jacob's death about Elisha's servant and the unseen forces, and how men of God saw what others could not or would not see. These men knew that God was on their side in the greatest of difficulties. They understood, as I was beginning to learn, that the unseen forces of God were more than a match for their adversaries.

I wanted the congregation to know what was sustaining us during this time. I prayed that they would see God's gallant horsemen, view His galloping horses, and hear His speeding chariots as the heavenly hosts arrived on the scene of their difficulties. I encouraged them to see His celestial warriors all around us and to know, really know, that all His power was there to help. If so, they would understand, as did Elisha, that God is not only able to

assist us, but He has provided an army that far out-
numbers the enemy.

"Between us and the forces of Hell is the everlasting
power of God," I said. "If we can grasp this truth, we will
be like Elisha—people of faith and confidence, people
without fear or panic." The strongest, bravest and most
fearless men, I observed, are those who believe in and lean
upon those heavenly forces.

Standing misty-eyed before my congregation, I wanted
them to know that it was not what the pastor said that
was important, but what he lived out. I hoped they would
see their pastor as he really was, and through this that
they would realize that what God was doing in my life He
desired for all His children. I did not want them to see me
as a spiritual giant, but as a hurting father in need of His
covering, His grace and His love. Apart from the grace of
God, I was so much like Elisha's servant—weak because
of what I did not see, gripped with fear because of what I
did not understand, ready to surrender because of overwhelming circumstances. Even so, I was still catching a
glimpse of God's invisible forces and was learning that
there is no problem or no circumstance too great for God.

"As Christians," I said, "we are not alone. God has
created others to stand with us. Psalm 34:7 says, 'The
angel of the Lord encamps around those who fear Him,
and rescues them' " (NASB). Angels, I was becoming more
and more aware, were not idle dreamers with no more to
do than to drift along streets of gold or float on white,
fleecy clouds and listen to the music of harps all day. They
were fully employed, working on our behalf. No power of
evil could avoid their observation. Wherever the enemy
lurks—whether in daylight or in darkest night—an angel
is watching, ready to come to our defense. The enemy may
press us hard; he may harass and threaten, trying to fill
us with fear. But when we pray, our heavenly Father

opens our eyes. He strengthens our hearts, and He lifts our spirits.

By the time the message was over that morning, I had conveyed what I truly believed — that I had seen the enemy and that he was no match for the all-encompassing power and comfort of God.

9

I'll Never Forget You, JJ!

Peggy

We arrived at the mortuary early that afternoon to spend a few minutes alone with Jacob before the two-o'clock viewing of his body. I was grateful for the privacy afforded by the double room. While the rest of our family gathered in the waiting area, Don and I led the boys quietly into the viewing room. We gently closed the double doors behind us and approached the casket.

"I love you, JJ," Donny whimpered. Catching sight of Jacob's bruises, he began to touch and examine his brother carefully. I couldn't help reflecting on the irony of this moment. After bringing Donny home from the hospital three years before, I had stripped him down to his nothingness and laid him on a blanket on the couch for Braxton and Jacob to examine. "Touch him and look him all over," I had encouraged. Now, Donny was inspecting his brother.

I scooped Donny into my arms and held him tightly as we stood looking down at our beloved Jacob. Sniffling from light sobs, Braxton slipped his arms around Jacob and kissed him on the cheek.

The fragrance of flowers filled the room with a subtle, comforting sweetness as Don tried in simple terms to explain Jacob's death. JJ was like a tiny grain of wheat which had fallen into the ground, he said. Its hard little shell had to die and break open so that the soft inside could live and grow and produce more life.

"That's what happened to Jakie," he said tenderly. "He's in Jesus' house now. This is only his shell . . . "

We had been urged by well-meaning people not to worry about how Braxton and Donny would take their brother's death. "Kids bounce back, they don't really comprehend — especially Donny," they said. But of all the children who would see Jacob that day and Monday, Donny was the most observant. He noticed in detail the bruises on his nose, his black eye, the puncture marks on his hands, the stitches behind his ear and on his throat, his shaved head under the surgical bandage — and the make-up. This bothered him the most.

As Don led us in a brief prayer, speaking of the day that as a family we would see our JJ again, Donny squirmed and stretched vigorously in my arms, impatiently rubbing the makeup off of Jacob. I tried to keep his hands off his brother, but it was futile.

As Braxton waited in solemn silence, Donny fired one question after another and explored Jacob's body from head to toe.

"Who cut JJ with a knife?"

"Why are JJ's eyes closed?"

"Who beat him up, Mommy?"

"Why did they put make-up on my JJ? Do they think he's a sissy?"

"Mamma, JJ has lipstick! Why does he have on lipstick?"

"What's wrong with his hands?"

They were swollen and folded over his Bible. Donny tried to move them, but we stopped him.

"How can he hold the Bible if he's not there, Mommy?"

"Can we take him home like that?"

"Has he got shoes on?"

Donny tugged on the lid of the casket to inspect the lower half of Jacob's body. "Yeah, he has got his shoes on . . . and his socks!" he exclaimed.

"Is Jacob wearing his underwear?"

It was hard for us to let him go through this meticulous examination of his brother, but we wanted him to feel satisfied. Don and I believed it was better for the boys to experience this part of life with their family, rather than to discover it with someone who may not have the patience or the understanding to answer their questions.

As Don explained about Jacob, I tried not to look. Jacob looked pale and, with the make-up covering his freckles, he didn't seem natural. Donny was persistent about removing the make-up. For a child of three, he had a fair understanding of who had done this to his JJ.

"Where is he?" he demanded about the mortician. "I'll get him!"

Jacob had watched over Donny all his life, and now it was Donny's turn to protect him. In his child-like way, he didn't want anyone to see his brother looking like a sissy. No matter how many times the mortician reapplied the make-up before the funeral, Donny would rub it off, leaving his little thumb print as evidence of his work.

Exhausted from holding onto this wiggling, twisting little boy, I put him down.

"Daddy, I want to kiss JJ," he begged. Don reached down and lifted him up. Donny bent low and planted the kiss.

His voice quivered. "I'll never forget you, JJ!"

As Don set him down again, he scampered toward the double doors yelling, "I'll get him. JJ's no sissy."

A member of our waiting family stopped him as he burst through the doors.

Don _____

Shortly before two o'clock, members of our congregation began to gather with our family for the viewing. One by one they silently filed by the casket. Although as a pastor I had been close to other members of our congregation in moments like these, I had not realized until now just how important these viewing sessions are to the family. People don't take off work to attend funerals as they once did. Many times I have conducted services at the request of a mortuary where only one or two people have shown up.

I was concerned on our part that because this was a holiday weekend, few would attend Jacob's memorial. Sunday's low attendance at the viewing heightened our concern. We felt alone. Not only had we lost our son, but Peggy was sick, we were unsettled in our new house, our home was whirling with visiting family and guests, and now it looked as though hardly anyone would show up for the funeral. On Monday, however, we began to discover just how many lives our little boy had touched.

Many of the visitors were children. Peggy ministered much of the day to them, helping to calm their fears about death. Although I loved and respected her for what she was doing, I resented the fact that my little boy was the guinea pig. Furthermore, knowing how much she loved Jacob, it was painful for me to see her so open and vulnerable as she allowed the children to touch him. I could never have done what she did; Jacob's death was too personal. The more I observed her love and patience with the children, however, the more I realized how much it meant to her.

Peggy _____

At first I took each child separately in to see Jacob, sometimes accompanied by the parents. Holding the children up so they could get a better look, I talked quietly.

"Are you afraid?" I asked. Most nodded their heads shyly. I tried to explain that Jacob was with Jesus and encouraged them to touch him. We talked about how much fun it was to play with him and what a joy it would be to see him in Heaven.

Like Donny, many of the children were full of questions.

"What do his hands feel like?"

"I don't know; let's touch them and find out," I would reply. Usually they were amazed at the coldness of his skin.

"How come they feel funny?"

"Because Jacob isn't there," I explained. "His body is like a house. It's warm when you're home, but when you're not—and the heater isn't on—it gets cold. The thing that makes the heat is what Jacob was inside, and that's gone to be with Jesus."

"How are you going to know it's him when he doesn't have his body there?"

That was a great question. "I don't know, but Jesus tells us that he's there, and that we will know Jacob the same way we know Him."

"When are we going to see him again?"

"When we go to Heaven," I smiled.

"Are we going there now?"

"Well, I don't think so, but we never know . . . 'cause we didn't even know when Jacob was going."

Sometimes when answering their questions, I could make the children laugh and giggle. This helped to calm their fears, and they would leave feeling calm and reassured. Many gave me a comforting hug.

This experience taught me that we must be completely open and honest with children about death. Fear of the unknown creates anxiety, sometimes terror. If we keep death a mystery, children will dread it.

The scary part of death is the tears and sorrow of those who are left behind. But in the midst of it all, there are lessons to be learned. Dying is part of living. Death is coming to all of us. To know about death as we know about life is healthy, and we need to give our children permission to ask all the questions they have about it. If all that children experience about death is pain and sadness, they will shrink from it. They must know that when it comes time for them to die—or for their mommies or daddies to go—they need not fear because death is a natural extension of life.

In the weeks to come I discovered just how important this truth is as several children shared visions and dreams they had had about Jacob. One little girl, Heather Cave, came up to me after a church service elated.

"Hey, Peggy! Guess what!" she beamed. "When we were praying today, I felt somebody was looking at me. I looked up and saw Jacob. He was watching us praying. I saw him!"

I wrapped my arms around her and hugged tightly. "You don't know how good that makes me feel," I wept happily.

On another occasion, a little boy in our church related a dream he had about Jacob. In the dream he was running, and as he looked behind him, he saw Jacob carrying a suitcase in his hands.

"I could tell he wasn't coming back," the boy whimpered. "He was walking away, and I don't understand that."

"Maybe, Danny, you were seeing Jacob packing everything and taking it to be with Jesus," I offered encouragingly. "Maybe the Lord was allowing you to see that he's not coming home again, and that he has a new home now."

"Oh, I get it," he smiled brightly. "So when I leave, I'm going to take everything and go there, too, huh?"

"That's it, that's going to be it, Danny."

These precious experiences may never have occurred had they regarded Jacob's death as some secret, hush-hush-or-you'll-make-Peggy-cry experience.

As I look back on that day of sharing with the children in the viewing room, I realize how God transformed a potentially long and painful ordeal into a dayspring of blessing. Like Donny, these children could say, "I'll never forget you, JJ."

10

The Warming of the Room

Don

It was not going to be easy to keep things in perspective. Already folks were calling Jacob's death a tragedy. And of those who were not, some felt that God had taken him to save us from future heartache.

They thought they were being kind when they said things like, "It's a good thing God took him because of what he could have been, an alcoholic or a drug addict"; or "Aren't you excited that he's in Heaven?"

Sometimes I just wanted to say, "That's not a very fair question."

I learned from this experience how little we all really know about ministering to the grief of others. Though well-meaning, their words of supposition cut razor sharp into my heart. *Don't they realize how much that hurts? Why don't they think before they speak?* I wondered. *Jacob was only six, hardly ready for Hell's Hall of Fame.*

As I questioned the wisdom of those who tried to comfort me, I was painfully aware of the many times I had visited the hospital or attended a family who had just lost a loved one – and uttered some of those same phrases. How hollow these cliches sound when we are in the depths of grief: "The Lord will provide"; "All things work together for the good"; "He's with the Lord now"; and so on. No matter how true they are, these platitudes do not fill the void left by the loved one.

Actually, I don't know that there is a lot a person could say that would help. Mostly what you need is a hug or a hand-holder or a listener. Probably the best thing a person could do is encourage you to talk about your loved one, because that's a way of keeping him real.

Healing comes in a moment-by-moment dependence on the grace of God as we put into practice His Word, "Let him have all your worries and cares, for he is always thinking about you and watching everything that concerns you" (1 Peter 5:7, TLB). All that we really need in grief is to know that someone cares and understands, and this is best expressed in a loving look, a tender touch or a helping hand.

Memorial services are vital occasions for such caring to take place. More than eight hundred people packed the church Tuesday morning for Jacob's funeral, overflowing onto the balcony stairs and into every available spot in the auditorium. Personal friends, members of our congregation, acquaintances from the community, the mayor, our family doctor, Jacob's karate instructor, his soccer and baseball teams – in every misty eye was the tender look of compassion.

"It is significant today that this service has been designated a worship service," my cousin Charlie Gregg began. "We've come together today as relatives and friends to help Don and Peggy seal a previously made covenant with

God. Six years ago at an altar not unlike this, they said, 'Lord this child is yours; we commit him to You.' And today, with great difficulty, yet with greater faith, they are affirming that covenant . . . ''

As Charlie spoke of the paradox of joy in sorrow when Christians lose a loved one, my mind raced over the years that Jacob had been ours. Charlie's words were deeply comforting. "Don and Peggy, the anguish that pierced your soul the night of Jacob's death, none of us can know. But as deeply as sorrow has wounded your heart, that deeply you can love each other. And as intensely as you have felt hurt over the loss of Jacob, that intensely you can be touched by the feelings of others' infirmities.

"When this sense of loss lessens, our memory that is now pain will become our pleasure because we will see Jacob for what he was . . . for what he gave to us. I am reminded today of God's favorite name in the Old Testament for Himself. Over and over again, it was a name that God seemed to revel in and enjoy. He said, 'I am the God of Jacob.' And I hold on to that today; He is the God of Jacob.''

"The God of Jacob" was a great source of comfort to our family, but I wondered whether the sense of loss would ever lessen. Peggy and I were committed to years of hurting and sorrow. I was therefore amazed by the message given next by my uncle George. "The healing of this family, as C. S. Lewis suggested, will come like the warming of a room," he encouraged. "The process is going on long before you realize it."

I had never thought of the healing process in that light. Everyone I had talked to had spoken of some time in the future when healing would begin its comforting work. Now, we were being told, that healing was already taking place. I wrote myself a mental note, *Tonight, when everything is calmed down, I'll think back over the past few days and remember all the love and concern that our family and many friends have shown us. George is right. Healing has begun.*

We had designed the memorial as a worship service. Each of the songs had special meaning to the Gregg family. Midway through the service, as the congregation concluded singing "Majesty," the beautiful song by Jack Hayford, Peggy stood with her eyes closed and hands raised. A startled hush fell over the audience as the words of a heavenly language flowed from her lips. Reverently, we waited for an interpretation to the message. When none came, the service continued.

I was the last to speak. Stepping toward the podium behind Jacob's casket, I was determined to focus on the triumph of his death. I chose each word carefully.

"This morning I want to share with you about Jacob's life, his death, and its affect upon each one of us today. The pain has been great for both Peggy and me," I sniffled, "but let me tell you this morning that God's grace has been more than sufficient. We have found a peace and have felt a strength far greater than the pain. To make sense of what took place on Wednesday of this past week, it's important that we look at Jacob's death as a triumph of God's power in every situation of our life. If we were to view our loss as a tragedy, we would lose sight of God's purpose in Jacob's life . . . "

Fingering my baseball glove which I planned to use in recalling happy moments in Jacob's life, I swallowed hard against the lump in my throat, then continued. "We don't believe that he was taken without a purpose. And it is our desire in this service today to tell you that God had a purpose, not only in Jacob's life, but in his death. It would be pointless to consider Jacob's life and death unless we were able to see some fruit."

That fruit, I observed, was a resurrection experienced in the hearts of those touched by Jacob's life. "There's been a recommitment in many of our lives toward seeing those we hold dearest to us in Heaven," I said. "Some who needed healing in their spirits received it this past Sunday, and many are receiving a resurrection today as we share part of Jacob's life."

I paused for a moment to adjust the microphone. Then, gazing at Peggy, I continued. "There was a resurrection in his mother's heart when she found strength to say to Jesus, 'He's yours,' and busied herself for six years, nine months and seventeen days preparing him for Heaven, and then in discovering that God is sufficient to keep that which she committed until the day when we will all be reunited.

"The harvest of Jacob's life is also found in his father who learned the very important lesson that church for children is not just babysitting. It is the preparation ground for eternity."

I spoke of the many cards and phone calls we had received, and of the ones we had hurt in fourteen years of ministry who had found the grace to put their arms around us in forgiving and comforting love.

"I thank God that through Jacob's life and death there is a resurrection in our spirits," I testified. "We sense a new goal and purpose in the calling that God has upon us. And today, Peggy and I share with you the joy of knowing that He is able to take the wreckage of our lives and to mold it into vessels of His glory.

"Now I would like for you to join with me in rededicating your lives to the purpose for which God created you. You may have children who don't know Jesus Christ as their Savior. God has entrusted them into your care for eternity. Jacob prayed for people who didn't know Jesus, and I want you to make that commitment to God and just say, 'Father, forgive me of my sins and help me to live my life the way you want me to live.' "

Concluding my message, I held my glove before the audience. "I don't have much to give my son," I stammered, fighting back a new flood of tears. "But I do have my glove. It was special in his life, just as it was special to me. My father bought it for me when I was thirteen years of age, and I have cherished it all of these years . . . "

Glove in hand, I stepped down and around the array of flowers to Jacob's side. As the organ quietly played his favorite chorus, "In My Life Be Glorified," I gently placed the glove on his folded hands, planted a last kiss on his cheek and stood quietly aside. Peggy rose hesitantly from her seat and approached. She paused beside Jacob, looking long and misty-eyed into his pale face. Then, bending low over the edge of the casket, she draped an arm over his form in a firm hug, kissed him long, and straightened. As she slowly turned to leave, I put my arms around her and we embraced, sharing an unashamed moment in silent sorrow.

I escorted Peggy back to her seat before the final processional began. The organ softly played children's choruses as one by one Jacob's many friends filed past, some lingering momentarily for a prolonged last glimpse, others to hug his daddy. Many stepped aside to comfort Peggy. One, a fellow minister, whispered into her ear. "God gave me the interpretation to your message in tongues, but I was hesitant to give it. Please forgive me. I'll write it down and send it to you so that you will have it as a remembrance of God's word to you."

When the letter arrived a few days later, I could tell by the expression on Peggy's face that it brought God's answer to an earnest prayer. She had asked God to let her see Heaven, hoping that in her vision she would catch a glimpse of Jacob. The message read, "If I should rend the heavens, the glory would be more than you could stand, for the splendor and joy (of Heaven) is beyond your imagination. Therefore, rejoice in what you know and cling to that which you understand, for in a short while I shall make the change that shall enable you to behold and enjoy that which I have prepared for all who love Me."

In those days following the funeral, we became more and more aware of the "warming of the room" as God's healing grace began its gentle work in our hearts.

One warming came while Peggy was still suffering from tracheitis. Until the infection cleared, the only way she could sleep was in a sitting position. Unable to get comfortable enough to sleep, she decided she would spend that time in God's Word instead. We had not had time to unpack since the move to our new home, and she could not find her Bible. As she searched through our belongings, however, she uncovered an old Bible that she had not seen before. Thumbing through its pages, she would select passages that would bring comfort and strength and then would read until she fell asleep.

On the fourth night after the funeral, memories of Jacob had left her in exquisite pain. Medleys of events drifted across her mind as she pictured Jacob. Although in her heart she knew Jacob was in the care of Jesus, thoughts like *Were you in pain? Are you cold? Where are you now? What are you facing when I can't be there to comfort you?* brought tears of distress. As she reached for that old Bible and drew it to her, a note fell out. Wiping a blur of tears from her eyes, she began to read. "When in trouble or overcome with distress, turn to Psalm 46."

Peggy flipped through the pages to the psalm. "God is our refuge and strength, a very present help in trouble," the passage began. "Therefore we will not fear . . . " Slowly, verse by verse, she read through the psalm. Suddenly, her heart jumped as the words in verse 7, "the God of Jacob is our refuge," seemed to leap from the page.

The phrase was repeated in verse 11, taking on special meaning as though God were speaking directly to her broken heart. Tears again filled her eyes and spilled down her cheeks. These, however, were tears of joy as the comforting peace of the Holy Spirit penetrated her mind and settled deep into her heart.

The next morning she was smiling and laughing.

"You're happy this morning," I observed. "I haven't seen you this way since the accident."

Peggy explained what happened. "Did you write that message down for me?"

I shook my head. "I didn't even know we had that Bible."

She handed it to me, and I remembered at once. It had belonged to Elizabeth Indart, an elderly lady in our church who had died the year before. After her death, several staff and board members of the church joined me in going through her personal effects. When I was asked if there was something of hers that I would like to have, I chose the Bible. I hadn't seen it since that day and had forgotten about it. When Peggy showed me the note, I recognized Elizabeth's handwriting.

We marveled that out of all the books we had, and the number of Bibles we had collected, the only one that she could find was Elizabeth's. Almost one year after her death, she, through her note, ministered warming words of triumph to Peggy's heart.

Just a few weeks later, we began to realize we soon would be facing our first Christmas without Jacob. It was October, and our church choir was preparing its sixteenth Annual Singing Christmas Tree program, which is attended by more than ten thousand people at seven performances over a five-day period. Jacob had been so much a part of the Tree that it wouldn't be the same without him, and I began getting depressed.

About that time, though, our music minister, Dan Burchett, came to me and said, "The Christmas Tree Committee was wondering if it would be all right with Peggy and you if we dedicate this year's Singing Christmas Tree to Jacob."

Stunned, I looked at him for a long moment, and then just nodded. None of them, not the choir, the Tree Committee, or Dan, knew how much I was hurting over the thought of going through that celebration without my boy—but God did. My heavenly Father once again had been warming the room before I felt it, and He provided a healing agent when I needed it.

Another warming, which we are still experiencing, began through the Royal Rangers, a youth ministry sponsored by the Assemblies of God, which had meant a great deal to Jacob. During Jacob's funeral, Col. Jim Price, director of the Royal Rangers for the Southern California District, announced a memorial fund "to help boys like Jacob come to know Jesus."

This Memorial Fund was established to raise money for various outreach ministries. One would be the Royal Ranger fort to be built up at Camp Pinecrest in the San Bernardino mountains. Designed something like the fort at Disneyland, it has a capacity of 300 to 400 youngsters. During the summer, kids can come to camp out, learn archery and woodsman-type skills like hunting, and have powwows (big get-togethers) in a campfire setting. Services are held giving these kids an opportunity to accept Jesus Christ as their Savior and Lord.

Some of the funds went directly to the District Royal Rangers to keep their program going, and some went to our local church to buy equipment for their campouts.

Other projects that have been helped by this fund are a missionary organization in Mexico for their training facility for pastors and their orphanage for children, the Youth With a Mission organization for their Early Childhood Development Center in Hawaii, and a car for a missionary friend of ours out of Texas who raises money for other missionaries.

The Memorial Fund continues to be active, reaching boys and girls for Christ, and it began at Jacob's funeral service. At the close of the service, two small boxes were placed in the foyer of the church for those who wanted to contribute. We were pleased to discover the next day that more than seven hundred dollars had been given.

In this memorial to Jacob, other members of our family also would find healing. Friday a member of our church came into my office and shared how Jacob had touched his life. "I want to do something to help keep his memory and influence on others alive," he offered.

"What do you have in mind?" I asked hesitantly.

"I want to give four times the amount of money that comes into Jacob's Memorial Fund within the next four weeks."

I was stunned. "Do you know how much has already come in?"

"No, but it doesn't matter. I want to do it," he insisted.

"Okay," I smiled. "I'll let you know at the end of the month how much comes into the account."

"But there are two conditions," he injected. "No one must know who the money came from, and payment must be made over the next four years. Each payment will equal the total amount given at the end of the month."

I shook his hand vigorously and thanked him for his generosity promising to carry out his wishes. As he left the office, I lifted my eyes and thanked the Lord for the impact that my little boy had had on that man. The knowledge that Jacob would live on and that his life would touch the lives of many other young boys, though they would never know him, again warmed the room of my heart.

The first week passed, and five hundred dollars came in. The fund now totaled twelve hundred. I went immediately to the man and asked incredulously, wondering whether he realized what he was getting into. "Do you know how much money is in the fund?"

"It doesn't matter," he assured, "The Lord has already told me how much it's going to be."

If you already know, why don't you just tell me? I thought. So I decided to ask him.

"Because God wants to teach you three things in these next few weeks," he explained patiently. "The first is that the amount of the funds will far exceed your expectations, and it will continue to grow even after the four weeks. The second is that the money for this fund will not come from sources that you expected it to come from, but from many people whom you have not met. The third thing God wants to show you is that the fruit of Jacob's life and death is just beginning and will continue for years to come."

He paused for a moment to let his words sink in, then continued. "I will hand you an envelope on Sunday with the amount that I will be giving. I want you to put it in a safe place and at the end of the four weeks, open it up and see what it will be."

The next three weeks dragged on day after day. Finally the moment came when I could open the envelope. First, I found out how much had come in during the month. The first lesson came true after the end of the second week. Contributions had exceeded fifteen hundred dollars — far more than I had expected. I realized then that God would not be limited by my lack of vision.

The final tally for the four-week period was twenty-five hundred. I quickly multiplied that by four and realized there would be another ten thousand dollars to add to the fund. Excited, I strode quickly into the bookkeeper's office, opened the safe and reached for the envelope. Hurrying back to my office, I sat at my desk and stared at the envelope for a few moments. Did the figures match? *No one would expect anyone to give ten thousand dollars. Whatever is in this envelope will be more than enough,* I thought, bolstering myself for what I feared might be a letdown.

Finally, I tore open the envelope and pulled out a folded piece of paper. Holding my breath, I unfolded it and read the message: "Ten thousand dollars to be paid in twenty-five hundred dollar increments over the next four years." Not one cent more or less than it was supposed to be. I couldn't believe it.

Amazed by this miracle, I decided to investigate further. Calling the bookkeeping office, I asked for a list of donors to Jacob's Memorial Fund. It was time for me to discover my second lesson. Just as the church member had predicted — and to my surprise — not one cent of the twenty-five hundred dollars had come from those whom I expected to give.

I am still learning my third lesson. From that first twenty-five hundred dollars, the fund has grown to more than $130,000 in just six years, half in donations from people who never knew Jacob, but who had heard about the kind of boy he was and wanted to keep his memory alive.

The healing spreads as the warming continues.

11

Not Missing the Little Things

The Friday after Jacob died Peggy and I stopped at the Karate school where Braxton and Jacob had trained for two years.

We walked into the studio, and Chong Kim, the boys' instructor, greeted us as he always did. He bowed his head in respect toward my position as a minister. Then he shook my hand, looked deep into my eyes, and asked, "What's wrong?"

I said, "Jacob was killed in an accident on Wednesday."

He was shocked.

Mr. Kim had invested a great deal of time, energy and love into our sons' lives. For one thing, he had attended some of the church functions in which the boys had been involved, and this let the boys know that they were special to him and that he was concerned about their lives.

That he really did care always stood out in our minds. Through his caring, he had become an extension of our

113

The boys loved karate. They went three to five times a week for lessons. Here's Jacob with his friend Bobby.

family. It was only natural that we wanted to let him know right away what had happened.

Overcome with grief, he put his arm around me and spoke words that I will never forget. "He's not your son now. He's God's son."

A simple statement. Yet these words were to open the door for Peggy and me to begin to live in the freedom of God's choice to take Jacob. All the questions, doubts, fears — and even anger at times — that would come later would be soothed somewhat by the words, "He's not your son now. He's God's son."

We say our children are God's children, but most of the time we don't treat them like they're God's kids. Those words of Mr. Kim's put the issue right out in the forefront, and we needed to hear them. They were a reminder of what we had really promised six years earlier when we dedicated Jacob to God. We had said, "Lord, He's Your child. He's not ours." Now, more than at any other time, we really had to believe what we had said, and it was as though the Holy Spirit guided that concept right to our hearts.

In thinking about this idea afterward, I remembered the day we brought Jacob to the church to dedicate him to God. It was a special moment in Jacob's life and in our own, and I felt proud as I looked down into his eyes. I began to imagine what he might become — maybe a doctor who would discover some new cure for humanity, or a lawyer defending the rights of an accused person, or possibly a professional baseball player. The last thing I wanted for Jacob was for him to become a preacher. There were too many demands, and not enough rewards like there would be for discovering the cure for cancer, or hitting a home run in the bottom of the ninth with the bases loaded and winning the game for your team. What could possibly compare to those feelings?

But that was when Jacob was my son. Now, I could see the difference. What does a cure for cancer mean if an individual still dies without Christ, or what good is a home run if the person loses the game of life? God was showing me that His son Jacob was still going to live, even in death, and make an impact in people's lives, sometimes even determining where they would spend eternity.

Probably the first life that Jacob, as "God's son," influenced was my own. I began to wonder what good would come out of my accepting that fact. It didn't take long for me to realize that if I accepted God's hand in our loss, I would ultimately see God's gain.

As the weeks and months passed, I noticed a real desire in my heart to draw closer to God. At first, it was because I wanted to be sure not to miss Heaven and my reunion with Jacob. As time passed, though, I became aware that I wanted to know more about God so that I could see what He would accomplish in Jacob's death. In other words, I didn't want to miss anything.

I began to feel like Elisha in 2 Kings 2:2 when the prophet Elijah thought the young man should no longer travel with him but should get established in the city where they were. He suggested Elisha stay there rather than go to Bethel with him.

I love what young Elisha said: "As the Lord lives and you, yourself live, I will not leave you." So they went down to Bethel together.

The thing that excited me about this (and still does) is that in essence Elisha was saying, "I've been too close to you and your ministry to just stay behind. Wherever you go, things happen. I've seen the miracles, felt the presence of God, and know the power of His Word. Tarry here? And let you go on without me? Never!" Elisha knew that if he stayed behind, he would miss what God was going to do through Elijah.

At each new stop, Elijah said, "Tarry here."

But Elisha always said, "I will not leave you." He was determined to be a part of what God was doing.

Elijah finally turned to his young charge and asked, "And what shall I do for you before I am taken from you?" In other words, "I see that you're not satisfied with just seeing the hand of God. You want to experience it in your own life. So what is it that you want from me?"

Elisha answered, "Please, let a double portion of your spirit be upon me. I want to be a part of what God is doing. I want Him to use me as He has used you."

That's the way I felt. I wanted to be as close to the fire of God as I possibly could. I was tired of being on the sidelines, hoping and wishing for something to happen. I was tired of being like the sons of the prophets who were satisfied with standing on top of the hill just watching God work. I desperately wanted to be used to touch others' lives with the good news of the gospel of Jesus Christ. This new feeling drove me to a sensitivity in my relationship with God that I had never experienced before.

I began keeping my eyes open for every chance I might have to share the miracle of what God was doing. As I became more receptive, and maybe even more trans-parent before God and before people, He opened more doors for me to share His great grace and mercy.

I was invited to speak at a number of banquets for the Royal Ranger Department of the Southern California District of the Assemblies of God. The opportunities to share the part this organization had played in shaping Jacob's life were exciting, but even more exciting was the fact that we were raising funds to build a fort in a Chris-tian camp to reach and teach — and keep — boys for Christ.

As these opportunities arose, God enlarged my vision for what He was going to do through this camp. One evening I rolled back the months to a night in May of 1982 when Jacob was five years old. I had taken him, along with Braxton, to a Royal Ranger campout. There the boys were taught how to pitch a tent, how to cook, and how to take care of themselves in the outdoors, but most important, they were taught to know and love the Lord. It was during one of the nightly services, after the message, that I saw my little boy respond to the altar call. I knew that at that young age he could hardly be classified as a hardened sinner, yet he did realize his need to know Jesus as his personal Savior.

As my mind went back to that night, I could still see, by the glow of the campfire, a Royal Ranger leader lay his hand upon Jacob and lead him in the sinner's prayer. I remembered with tears of joy the excitement in Jacob's voice as he later shared his experience at the campfire with three men, Colonel Jim Price, the head of the Southern California group, Robert Jiminez, a Royal Ranger leader, and myself. I had been proud of his decision—and in awe of his excitement. And now, at this banquet, God was giving me the opportunity to relate to others what the organization meant to us. I knew that would help to provide a place where other boys' lives could be changed and their eternity settled—and God was doing it through Jacob.

As I prepared to share at another banquet, I noticed three small boys standing in the doorway of the dining hall. They reminded me of some of those little fellows Charles Dickens wrote about—clothes that were worn and tattered, no shoes, and dirt all over their faces, but their eyes gleamed as they began to ask questions about the banquet. "What's going on?" "Are you going to eat?" "Can we come in?"

I could see the wheels turning in their heads, and I laughed at their mischievous smiles that reminded me so much of Jacob.

Well, when you begin helping with fund raisers, you learn quickly that kids don't have money. You want to fill your banquet tables with adults—the more adults, the greater your opportunity to meet your financial goal. So what these children were asking was simply out of the question. *Why, they probably couldn't even pay the $6.50* *it costs to get in to the dinner,* I thought, and tried to turn my attention elsewhere and forget them.

But I couldn't get my mind off the situation. The more I pondered it, the more I felt God saying, "Open your eyes. You said you didn't want to miss anything, but if you keep looking at things the way you have in the past, you're going to miss what I want to do." I was taken back by that.

I had grown cocky. My eyes were open — hadn't I already seen God's hand upon this ministry? But I suddenly became aware that He was going to use Jacob's story in a different way that night, and if I weren't careful, I really would miss it.

The Lord quickly showed me that those three boys were the key, and I needed to keep my eyes on them. *But how? They can't afford to attend the dinner,* I thought. By now I had lost sight of the boys so I looked, and when I found them I invited them to be my guests for the dinner.

"Can we bring our daddy?" one asked with a big smile.

"Sure," I said nobly and gave him a fatherly pat on the head.

Half an hour later, after everyone had been served and the guests were chatting around the table, the three boys and their father wandered in, found a place to sit, and quietly began to eat their dinner. The boys were still dirty. Their father was dressed much like his sons, and I began to have misgivings. I thought, *What did I get myself into this time?*

During the service that followed the dinner, I tried to determine the right approach for describing the need to build a camp where young boys could find Jesus as their personal Savior. I could talk about all the problems that children face — broken homes, drugs, alcohol, abuse. Any one of these would be a good selling point, but I needed to know what God wanted me to say.

I prayed for direction, and the Lord impressed me to focus on those boys and their daddy. So I watched intently. I noted their movements, listened to them speak, and saw how much they loved each other. At the same time, I realized something was missing. The more I watched, the more I became impressed with a need—but what was it? And how could we meet it at a fund-raising banquet?

My eyes were still blind to the need when the words of Mr. Kim came to me: "He's not your son now. He's God's son." As I pondered that thought, excitement jumped up within me and I was certain that God was going to use Jacob to perform a miracle.

When Jim Price introduced me, he shared a little bit about how much Jacob loved Royal Rangers. He related how Jacob had spent one evening in Jim's tent eating watermelon and candy with his "friend, Colonel Price." Jim also mentioned that he had been my Sunday school teacher when I was a child and had watched me grow in the Lord. I thought, *If he only knew the struggles I've had these past few months to grow and stretch the way I should have in those early years . . .*

Then I stood to speak, knowing God was going to do something special. I told of the loss of Jacob and how comforting it was as a parent to know that Jacob knew Jesus as his personal Savior. When Jacob walked through his valley of the shadow of death, he was not walking toward a stranger, but a friend named Jesus. No one needed to introduce the two, for they were already well-acquainted. With this thought, my tears began to flow, the tears of a father who understands the joys of Heaven and possesses the peace of knowing that his child is being taken care of there. I closed the service with my final point, the need to provide a place where boys from the age of five through their teens could find a relationship with Jesus like Jacob had. I remarked that too many of our Royal

Ranger parents didn't know the Lord, and that it was such a tragedy when the boys couldn't learn about Jesus at home. Our responsibility was to fill that gap as much as we possibly could by providing this facility.

Two things happened that night that I shall never forget. First, we raised four thousand dollars more than we expected. That was a thrill for all of us.

Second, the father of those three boys came to me after the service and said, "I need to give my life to Jesus Christ." I never dreamed anyone would want to give his life to Jesus while we were trying to raise money, yet here he was, asking me to pray the sinner's prayer with him. Talk about excitement! Tears were running down his cheeks, and mine as well. Both of us knew that at that moment God had opened our eyes to His plan for our lives.

During the two-hour drive home, while I was thanking God for the marvelous results in the service that night, it dawned on me that if I hadn't listened when God said, "Open your eyes," I would have been content with just making the goal — and I would have missed His real purpose in the meeting! And then I wondered, *How many times have I missed the real purpose of a service by being satisfied with much less than what God wants to give?*

I also asked myself, *How many times in Jacob's young life did I miss what God was doing through him in touching other lives?* For instance, Jacob, along with Braxton, would go throughout the congregation each Sunday night before service and shake hands with everyone, smiling and saying hello. I didn't realize what that meant to people until after he was gone.

Another example was the times, twice a month, when Jacob, Braxton and Peggy would go to rest homes and visit each room. They would pray and sing for those elderly folks and generally just bring some joy into their lives. I'm ashamed to say that I didn't realize the impact that those things, which seemed like little things to me, had on people. I was so caught up in other things that I hadn't opened my eyes to the needs around me. Somehow, I believe God was trying to teach me, even then, that as long as I thought of Jacob as mine, I was going to continue to miss the "little" things.

It was — and is — those "little" things that are important in the kingdom of God. I had just finished preaching one Sunday evening, and people were responding to the altar call. At this time, as people are kneeling in prayer, I move among them and pray with each one individually. On that particular evening, Jacob came to me with tears in his eyes and asked me to pray with him.

I looked down at those teary eyes and said, "Sure."

These are probably the biggest highlights of my life — the opportunities I have to pray with my children, not because I say we should, or I force them to pray, but because they want to pray.

I knelt to pray with Jacob, and he threw his arms around my neck and began to tell Jesus how much he loved Him and how thankful he was to have Christian parents, loving brothers, and a church that he loved. By the time he was through, I could do nothing more than just hug him, plant a kiss on his cheek, and tell him how proud I was of him.

Jacob walked away with a big smile and said, "Thanks for praying with me, Daddy."

That moment was very important, but, as usual, I thought it was just something between Jacob and his daddy . . . just a little thing.

Someone else was watching, though, and that little thing became a big thing in her life. The woman came to me after Jacob died, and to my amazement, she told me how much it had meant to her to know and see the mutual love between her pastor and his son. It was something she would never forget. She spoke of changes that had taken place in her life as a direct result of what she saw that night.

Have you ever stopped to think how many of the blessings of God we really miss by trying to gauge what is important to us and what is not? As a preacher, I know that at times when people ask how many came forward for salvation on a particular Sunday, I wish there had been twenty or thirty who responded so it would look like I really was doing the job, and that God's blessings really rested upon my ministry. Too often, I think, we forget that God and all the angels and saints in Heaven get excited when just one person gets saved. The question is, If they get excited, then why don't we? I think it's because we get caught up in what we think are big things and miss the treasures that God tries to give to us in the small.

If there is anything that I've learned in releasing Jacob to God, it is that when I keep my eyes open like a child, I can see what God is doing and be a part of the changes He makes through Jacob.

The first changes I noticed were in me.

12

Changes

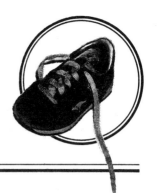

"Don't get too close to your people," one of my professors told me. "You can get near, but not close."

I was in training for the ministry, and those who seemed to know assured me, "It's not wise to put all your cards on the table. You need to maintain a suitable degree of aloofness."

I listened carefully to that advice—and through the years built a relationship with my congregation that was mostly surface.

A certain sense of confidence generally comes with time spent in the ministry, and it should give a pastor a deeper sensitivity toward people, but I allowed it to develop pride and arrogance in me.

In addition, I became degree oriented. If you wanted to succeed, you had to go to school, you had to progress, you had to have this degree and that degree. You had to stay on the edge of improving yourself—and you never finished.

Soon after Jacob's death, though, some things began happening to me. All the things I had built up — the aloofness, the self-confidence, the desire to be in control — just seemed to go down the drain. There was nothing left.

Then the Holy Spirit brought a Scripture to my attention that shed great light on what was going on. "Unless a grain of wheat falls into the ground and dies, it remains alone; but if it dies, it produces much grain" (John 12:24). When the grain of wheat is put into the ground, it loses its own identity and gives up its own previous existence. The rain comes, and the hard, outer shell begins to soften under the pressure; the secret life buried inside the kernel begins to swell and eventually splits the shell and cracks it open. Only then, after the individual grain is destroyed, can it multiply and send forth abundant fruit. Life rises out of apparent death, and the fruit brings blessings to all those it reaches.

When I read this Scripture, and thought about it, I realized that God had started to break down my pride, and my hard, outer shell was cracking. I began to understand that only as my life was broken before the Lord could what was really inside of me ever come out to benefit anyone beyond myself.

God showed me that a higher education did not make me any better Christian, or better preacher, or better teacher, or better servant. Rather, He would make me all those things when I allowed Him to saturate my life. If I would let Him, He would get past the exterior, into the interior, and release the real me. But I had to become vulnerable. If I were to be effective, I would have to get close to people, and let them get close to me. They would have to know me in a way different from before.

To allow the shell to break, I had to allow the pain. But eventually I could say to my people, "Here's who I am and what I am. I want to walk with you—talk with you. I want my spirit to meld with yours so we can grow together."

The breaking of the shell was not immediate for me—it happened over a long period of time. In fact, it is still going on. One area breaks off and I advance somewhat in my Christian walk, and God begins to work on another part. He puts a new hunger and thirst into me—more than I ever dreamed possible—and my life and ministry continue to expand.

My ministry never had been just a job to me—I have always ministered out of love—but the love is so much more real now. And I feel the love of the people for me. I respect them and we have a close, intimate bond.

When I speak about hurts, it's out of my own heartbreak. I weep with people because I share their feelings. When I counsel someone, I am personally committed because of what I've been through.

On the other hand, when I talk about hope now, and about the protective hand of God, I can express it with absolute assurance because it's something I have experienced fully. And the people feel it with me. Our relationships reach a depth that was impossible prior to Jacob's accident.

Peggy _____

Someone told me once about a certain woman who was said to have "compassionate eyes." When a stranger asked the woman's friend what that meant, the friend answered, "She is sensitive to people's hurts and to their pain."

The stranger then asked one of the woman's children, "How can your mother be so compassionate?"

The youngster answered, "The only way she got those eyes was through pain and sorrow."

That's kind of the way I feel. I have been brought to a caring that I was separated from before because of lack of experience. No one is prepared to handle that kind of pain — there is just no sense of readiness in your spirit. You break. Then the Lord begins to pour in His healing balm, and along with the breaking comes caring. It draws you closer to anyone else in pain.

A few weeks after Jacob died two young Spanish brothers were playfully scuffling over a gun. One of them accidentally shot and killed the other. I visited the mother.

I knocked on the door of their house, and when she answered, I said, "I heard you lost a son."

She answered, "I no speak English."

I said, "I lost a son." She couldn't understand me so I showed her a picture of Jacob, and said again, "I lost him; he's gone."

Then she understood. She began to weep and invited me in.

She could sense my loss, and she knew I felt hers. Though we didn't understand each other's language, the depth of our communication through touching and caring was amazing. I visited her a number of times, and after the first time her husband was there, too. He spoke English, and during one of our visits he interpreted a little, but he wasn't very communicative. He had suffered great shock and was in the stage of anger.

The situation was tragic. I would write down Scriptures for the mother, and touch her, and hold her, and let her know that I understood because I had experienced the same thing.

Another time, about a year later, I went to the hospital to visit a friend of mine who was in intensive care. As I went in, I noticed a Spanish couple sitting in the waiting room, looking very bewildered. I went on in to see my friend, but just before I left the area, I noticed a little Spanish boy lying in one of the beds. Reaching the waiting room again, I stopped and asked the couple, "Is your little boy in the intensive care unit?"

"Yes. He's been in a car accident," they said.

"I just saw him, and it looks as if he's sleeping comfortably," I smiled. "I can understand some of what you're going through. I had a son who was in intensive care."

I didn't tell them that Jacob had died — I didn't think they needed to hear that just then.

We talked very little, because in these situations talk doesn't do much good. But I wept with them, and asked, "Can I pray with you?" I was able to comfort them and they felt my caring.

I have always been sensitive to people's pain, but now I understand more clearly the depth and intensity of it. You feel you are drowning in it. You can't get away from it and no one can relieve it — but to have someone there with you, sitting beside you, or just holding your hand, is a tremendous support. I really feel fortunate to have this deeper sensitivity to those who hurt.

To me, Jacob was the grain of wheat. God chose to place him in our midst to touch all of us, and then when he died our lives were enriched because we all were brought closer to the Lord.

Don _____

When the fruit from the grain of wheat reached the congregation, the atmosphere of the church was transformed. In the immediate aftermath of Jacob's death, people seemed to feel that this whole experience was "holy ground." They began praying differently, and for different things.

A church is somewhat like a family, and the pastor seems to be the head of this "family." His own family becomes a very real part of the overall church family. And our people felt this loss keenly—everyone lost a member of his family. The church hasn't been the same. The people began to learn how to hold up someone who is hurting, how to care, love, nurture, and help in restoring and healing people who have been broken.

It was a new experience for them. One man said, "I always saw the pastor as the iron man."

And a woman said, "He is the one who always held together, and always stood strong for everyone else in their weakness."

You don't often see the pastor and his family broken. Their response showed us how much they really cared.

It had been easy for us to be a little hardened and indifferent toward the people. Sometimes I even said, "They want, and want, and want—and they don't really want to give."

I suspect that's true to a certain degree with some churches today because pastors are not as dependent on their people for food, clothing and other needs as they were years ago. The people don't have much opportunity to give, and they're not used to it. But when Jacob died, our people grabbed the opportunity to help us, and God blessed them and expanded and stretched them to heights they never before attained.

The people changed in another way, too. They became aware of how quickly death can come. We're not so surprised when it happens to adults, especially as they get older, but it is a shock when someone so young and so healthy, is taken so quickly—without any real rhyme or reason.

The people began to realize their own lack of preparedness, and they thought about their own family situations. They recognized that something could happen in the twinkling of an eye, and they saw just how quick a twinkling of an eye is . . . in the morning he was there, and in the evening he was gone. It heightened their sensitivity to how fragile life really is.

Our people also became acutely aware of the needs of other children—both in our church and outside. They realized how important the ministries to children and the programs they provide for them were. It was obvious that our teachers and leaders recommitted themselves in a more personal way to their ministries. They demonstrated a freshness of spirit and a newness of consecration to the positions they had been called to.

When Len Gottschalk, the man who directs our Royal Rangers, heard about the accident, he took his lunch hour and went to a quiet, private place.

He told me, "I was so hurt over the death of Jacob that I just sat for a long time. Then I began praying, and as I talked with the Lord, I began to feel such a burning for our young boys. I realized that I had been taking things for granted. Going every week sometimes makes it seem like work—it gets to be a burden. But this has brought home to me that you never know when these kids are going to be called home, or if they are ready. It made me see clearly the importance of ministering to the children in our church."

Another difference I noticed was that immediately after Jacob's death, our altar calls had much more depth to them. People came with a greater commitment, and more people were saved. Some of the people answered altar calls as a direct result of what they heard and saw in our lives. They thought, *If God can provide for you in this situation, maybe He can provide for us.*

We've watched some grow, and we've watched some struggle—but they still hang in there. A spirit of healing began then, and we still see it.

Even some couples who thought they had insurmountable problems and were seriously considering divorce were changed. Jacob's death, and the way God helped us to handle the situation, had said something to them. They realized that no problem was too great, no circumstance so difficult that God couldn't provide for them. At least three couples re-evaluated their situations and resolved them. In fact, when one of the couples came to talk with us, we were shocked that they were having problems. We hadn't realized anything was wrong. But something concrete happened in their lives—we saw it and we have watched it grow through the years.

I believe Jacob's death became a major part of people's personal lives, partly because they could see us going through what we had walked them through before. They desperately wanted to know how we would handle something like that, and our glass-bowl experience showed them.

As the people changed individually, the church, as a unit, changed as well. It has become united on many, many fronts. The first indication was their coming together in a common cause to pray for Jacob the night of the accident. They didn't know if he would live or die, and, beginning with the sixteen men on the elders' prayer chain, people got on the phone. The effort expanded until nearly the whole congregation had united as a body to pray for us.

We had scheduled a picnic for the following Sunday afternoon, and after the accident it was cancelled. But the people felt it was important to meet and pray for the pastor and his family. It had not been easy to get them together for a single purpose before, but that night they did it themselves—they held a united prayer service. There was no other pretense for that meeting.

Another decision they made that day was to help us with the financial load that had fallen on us. Everybody responded, and they all had a personal part in meeting the expenses.

On top of everything else, Peggy and I had made arrangements to move that weekend, and those plans couldn't be changed. The congregation organized various groups to handle the different jobs connected with that. One group packed, another group moved what had been packed, another group put up wallpaper, another cleaned up outside, and some painted—they did everything that needed to be done. Being drawn together for the one purpose of helping us in a time of deep hurt taught them the difference between saying, "I'll pray for you," and actually doing something to meet the needs. It showed them that there are many ways you can help people.

The day of the funeral a great number of people were involved. They put on a dinner for the family, and they all worked hard. Some took care of the flowers, and others helped with the many details at the funeral home. Again, everything we needed to have done was done.

Somewhere along the way, our church realized there would be a grieving period for us, a time we would not be able to function properly. Different groups formed to take whatever load I had as a pastor upon their own shoulders. In the process, the staff, the board of trustees and the board of elders all assumed new responsibilities. It was wonderful to see how they were drawn together by the creative power of the Holy Spirit. None of us had walked through that valley before. We had all done different things for different people at different times, but never so many things all at once. None of us knew how. No one person ever "directed traffic," but many different people said, "Well, this needs to be done, so let me get on it." God raised up a person for every need, and the people were mobilized.

This showed all of us what a church is really supposed to be, and what it can be. Since then we have had a hunger to learn even more ways to minister to people. We have never felt satisfied. The feeling seems to be, "Yes, the pastor was hurting. That was obvious. But how many other people are hurting that we're not aware of, and how can we become more sensitive? How can we be of real help?"

During the last several years—even before Jacob died —we have emphasized four things: forgiveness, mercy, healing and restoration. His death has made these things vital and alive in our people. The church has become a healing agent. They really hurt for people, and they hurt *with* people. They have developed a maturity in which they do not judge—they move immediately to the task of finding a way to help meet the need.

This desire to meet needs has been so intense that we recently established a fund to help underwrite a camp for abused children. I don't think that would have been possible if we hadn't been sensitized by the death of a child as to just how precious these formative years are.

I know this sense of ministry is still continuing because word of appreciation still comes to us from people who have been on the receiving end. For example, a man who had a death in his family and some hard circumstances to deal with said to me just a few weeks ago, "I never imagined a church could care enough to do what those people did."

A ripple effect continues to go out and touch others' lives. Someone asked, "Why is Bethany Church concerned about these things?"

And the answer is, "The pastor had a boy and that boy was the picture of life. Then one day he was, and one day he was not. Because of that we are aware that these things are going to happen, and we want to be sensitive."

Not only has the fruit from that one grain of wheat changed us and our church, but it also has changed the whole city. Well, maybe not the whole city, but certain areas of community service have seen change. The people at the florist shop and the funeral home expressed their involvement more as though Jacob were a member of their family rather than just a part of their business. Those who were active with both Little League and the soccer teams were deeply affected, too. Their concern for the young people and for what they are doing with them is deeper and broader. They take their efforts much more seriously than they did before.

Even the mayor's life was changed. I had spoken to him only twice before in the four years we had been in Alhambra, but he attended the funeral and eventually gave his heart to Christ. Our relationship with the mayor created a number of opportunities to witness to people in the community. When he introduced me, he would say, "I met this man just after his son died."

The inevitable questions always followed. One man responded with, "That's my worst nightmare — if something happened to my kid, I don't know if I could handle it. How did you handle it?"

And I had a chance to tell him.

Another person who was affected was a reporter from the Alhambra Post Advocate newspaper. He had been assigned to interview me about the historical significance of our church. He was intrigued with its rich history and the powerful effect it had had upon our community. He asked about my background and education, and he wanted to know how a young man of 32 could be leading this kind of church. As I responded, he continued his questions, each becoming more personal. Finally, he asked the question that changed his mind about what he should write about Bethany Church of Alhambra.

"Dr. Gregg, how many children do you have?"

"Three," I answered proudly, instinctively. It had been only days since Jacob's death, and I had not yet trained myself to think of having only two boys.

The reporter's next words were, "I see pictures on the wall and other things in your office that tell me there is another story here. What's going on?"

I told him briefly about Jacob's death, and he immediately began to question me about it. "How did you respond to that? It must be extremely difficult for you to stand in front of people all the time and not be able to show your real feelings. What do you do?"

"Yes, it is difficult to carry on, but I don't try to hide my real feelings," I said.

"Aren't you and your family different when you are alone?"

"No, we couldn't do anything in private that we were not doing in public," I smiled. "We knew we couldn't fake it because our feelings were too deep. We were too emotionally involved to be able to draw any secret line."

"How do you handle your anger? Don't you maybe kick dirt at God a little bit? Aren't you really, deep down inside, bitter toward God?" he probed.

His inquisitiveness told me these questions came from more than curiosity. I suspected he thought he might feel this way if he were in this situation, and he was afraid.

I answered, "Yes, we were angry with God for a while. That is a normal stage of grief. But God has given us victory in that area."

"But God didn't answer your prayers. Was that proper? If this religion, this thing you have, is really real, when you are doing the work of God, doesn't He protect His children? How do you feel about that?"

I didn't want to get into a theological discussion because I sensed that was not what he wanted. I just tried to explain our position as simply and clearly as I could.

Then he asked, "Is there anything in your mind that makes you doubt whether there is anything after the grave? Is there any reality there?"

"That's what we put our hope in," I assured him. "Without Christ there is no hope, and the apostle Paul says in the Bible that without hope we'd be the most desperate people in the world. But we do have Christ. And everything we have is based upon the fact that we do believe in Heaven. There is an afterlife. There is something beyond the grave—there is something to look forward to, and that is to be in the company of the Lord and those departed loved ones who have gone on before. Our hope is in the fact that we will be with our son again someday."

I am not sure if the reporter ever came to know Christ as his Savior, but he had to be influenced by what is clearly taught in God's Word. I pray for that man, and I thank God for the opportunity to tell him about God's love in our lives.

The grain of wheat has been buried, but we have learned to nurture and water that little grain, and fruit continues to come forth. We cling to the promise and watch for the harvest as we allow God's sovereignty in our lives. All the things we loved and remember about our little Jacob live on and continue to produce life—and changes—in others, and we derive great comfort from that.

Many of the changes were brought about without any effort on our part, but many others were directly affected by the choices we had to make. Some of those were very difficult.

13

Choices

Many years ago, in England, a church member asked his preacher to speak to his niece who was losing her sight. When the preacher came to her room, he found her crying. Between sobs she said, "I'm going to lose my sight and I'm never going to be able to see. I'm going to lose it. I'm going to lose it. What can I do?"

The preacher answered, "Well, honey, you have a choice. You can give your sight away, or it can be taken from you. You can make the choice."

"What do you mean?" she sniffled.

"If you give it away, you release it. But if it is taken, you lose it, and that always brings resentment."

When we went in to see Jacob for the last time, we were aware that we had to make a choice as to how we would handle the situation. We could give Jacob up, or he could be taken from us. One meant that we would release him. The other meant we would lose him.

If we had allowed bitterness to walk into that room with us, Jacob would have been taken from us. No matter

139

how we would have tried to spiritualize it later, in the depths of our spirits we would have felt we had lost.

The devil took his best shot, but he did not *take* Jacob. We chose to *give* him to Jesus. Therefore, though we have suffered just about the most extreme pain a person can bear in life, that of losing a child, we're not beaten down. We can stand up straight and say to Satan, "You did not win. We have found peace."

We believe that God just picked Jacob up and planted him someplace else. And we gave Him the right to do that.

From the very beginning we realized we would have to make our own choices. There were so many things that nobody could decide for us. In fact, nobody even knew what choices we would have to face. No one could even imagine the things that would confront us.

For example, the night Jacob died, someone in the room made the comment, "Well, you know, 75 to 80 percent of the marriages where a child dies end up in divorce."

Through everything that went on that night, and for weeks afterward, that statement stayed in the back of my mind and I wondered, *Are we going to be one of those statistics?*

As I look back now, though, I realize that, right at that time, God began a process of cementing Peggy and me together. It started with our embrace when the doctor told us Jacob was not going to live. We made an immediate, intense, unspoken commitment to each other to be supportive no matter what happened, and then we went in and sealed it at Jacob's side.

At times, after that night, I would sometimes wonder, when neither of us knew what the other was feeling or thinking, if the cement were cracking. I would ask myself, *Are we drifting apart? Are we being* driven *apart?* But then before long, understanding would come and our relationship would be strong again.

*Peggy*_____

You have to decide quickly what you really want. A lot of times in our society you can put off, you can avoid, you can run away. But that night we had to make immediate choices. We couldn't run away from them.

The first conscious choice I had to make when I walked in the door of the hospital was whether or not to blame someone for everything that was happening. I made a conscious choice not to place blame.

From then on I had to make deliberate choices each step of the way. The second one was to give Jacob up instead of letting him be taken.

Then Don and I each had to ask ourselves, and we had to have immediate, definite answers: Do I want my family to fall apart? Do I want to lose my other children as well as the one I gave up? Or do I want us to pull together as a couple? Am I willing to fight for that?

You do have to fight for some things, and one of them is unity, because it's not natural. A lot of times we had to struggle to stay together. It wasn't easy. We had to be vulnerable. We had to be humble. We learned to choose those attitudes.

The next conscious choice I made was to set a goal for myself: I determined we would *not* be one of those statistics. I would keep my family together no matter what I had to do, even if I had to set my own grief aside and care for them, wait on them hand and foot, in their grief. We were going to stay together.

I'm glad God gave me the power to make that choice then. It helped me later.

A few months after Jacob's death, Donny was badly mistreated by someone. That devastated us. Choosing to take a positive action then was the hardest choice I ever had to make. I chose to tell the person that because the Lord loves him, I love him, and I would forgive him because that's what I wanted Jesus to do for me. I didn't want to do this, but I believe the strength we had gained through Jacob's death allowed us to say, "Lord, You handled that, so You can handle this. There will be consequences; there always are. But we will approach it positively. We will forgive."

When things happen that you can't control, you have to make conscious choices. Satan wants you to pull away from God, and from each other, and he fires all kinds of darts at you. And sometimes the Lord stands aside and allows some of those darts to strike you. Then you have to make the choice and say, "I'm going to serve the Lord. I have to respond to these things in a Christ-like manner." It's when you don't respond that way that you are in danger of becoming one of those statistics.

For us, it seemed we would come to a crossroad, and whenever we made our choice to react as we felt God would have us to, we would grow in leaps and bounds as a family.

One day at church I stood with everyone and listened as the congregation sang, "All to Jesus I surrender; All to Him I freely give." Hurting deeply inside, I looked around and wondered, *Do you people realize what you are really saying? Do you understand that when you have to give it all, all means everything, or it's nothing?* I realized then that at some point in my life I had begun just to mouth the words, not really meaning what I was saying.

I even used to pray, "Lord, if my children are not going to serve You when they're older, take them when they're young . . . " That day I realized I couldn't say, "All to Jesus

. . . " so I made a conscious choice not to sing that song anymore. I knew I would really have to lay myself down, and I didn't think I could do that.

Eventually, when I looked at other choices I had made and at how faithful the Lord was when I made the right ones—I hadn't become bitter, our family was still together, and the Lord continued to carry us—I finally realized I could make that choice, too. Now I can sing that song, and I mean it from the depths of my heart. I will give it all.

Don _____

We were going through so much, one thing right after another, that we had to choose all along not to let any of those things defeat us.

Even now the devil still fights us—he fires bullets at us every day. The whole process of grief can be heavy, but we continually choose to accept the good and reject the bad. There are a lot of negatives we could pick out, but that's not where God has brought us. Whenever those negative thoughts come up, I am prepared, because we cemented it from the beginning when we sealed Jacob by *giving* him to God.

We determined then never to refer to Jacob's death as a tragedy. We made that statement during the funeral, "If you accept it as a tragedy, then you take away whatever God is going to do in the situation." And we refuse to believe that God would let that boy leave us without bringing about something good.

Each day we say, "I consciously choose to have victory *today* over Jacob's death." We don't know what tomorrow will bring until it comes. I do know that when I get up tomorrow morning, the first thing I will say is, "Lord, I thank You for today's victory over Jacob's death." And no matter what I'm going to face, it is not going to take that victory away from me.

We have to deal with the entire framework of our lives that way. We choose first and foremost to serve God. The Lord was sufficient for the first step, and for the next step, and for the next. Through Jacob's death, we learned that He can be our sufficiency for all things.

When our church members and others who were affected by our boy's death made the changes we mentioned earlier, they were making their choices as well.

The father who told me he almost lost everything when he heard that Jacob died couldn't believe God would take Jacob. He thought that so few others had the potential Jacob had. But at that time, that father realized it could have been one of his own. He chose to recognize and appreciate how precious they were.

Then the Royal Ranger leader came to me and said, "I realize every Sunday that maybe the boys I lead don't know Jesus the way Jacob did. The reality is that it could happen to any of them any time — and I have to do my best to make sure they are ready. I am making it a priority of my life." He made his choice, too.

Another man wrote me a letter recently. He had seen Jacob's shoe in my office, the one he wore the day he was killed, and this man had asked me about it. His letter said, "You know, Don, I've asked the Lord to let me know how you feel because I know it hurts you deeply." That was a courageous choice for him to make.

His letter went on, "I never quite understood how you felt. But the other day I was carrying my little one's tennis shoes up the stairs. I looked at them, and with a jolt I realized — they were empty. I was stabbed right then with how you must have felt." He went on, "I had to go into my boy's room and take him in my arms and hug him—and just assure myself that he was there. The pain was so great."

*Peggy*_____

People come to us sometimes and say, "We can't believe the way you are handling this situation. How can you do it?"

The question isn't whether you can handle it or not, because you have to. You either handle it wrong—or you handle it right. You make the choice. You see your true nature very quickly. I was surprised at how we handled it. I hadn't known how strong our commitment really was or how much God would uphold us.

We have to be willing to accept the reality, and people often are not. They can't believe that when someone is serving God a thing like this can still happen.

Our story traveled with the speed of light, it seemed. Someone in a doctor's office told it, and the person she told it to shared it with someone else, and she shared it with one of the patients who was a member of our congregation. The lady said, "You won't believe it, but we just heard that a pastor in the area lost his son, And this is what happened . . . "

And the patient said, "Oh, no! That's our pastor." Then she told someone else, who told someone else, and that person began relating the story to me, and it was us!

We tend to think we should have some type of high priority protection. We, ourselves, even questioned in the beginning, "Look what we're doing. How can this happen when we're ministering to Your people?" When something like this happens, we wonder what we did wrong. We said, "Things like this just don't happen to people who try to serve the Lord as best they can. There must be something that we're not aware of that's standing in the way. What are we doing wrong?" Then we have to deal with guilt as well as grief, and that can be nearly unbearable.

It's hard for people to accept a death like this, because when they see that it can actually happen to a pastor and his wife, they know it could certainly happen to them. Then they begin to look inward and ask themselves, "Where am I spiritually? Could I handle that if it hit me?" And they realize, "If not, I had better start preparing myself." And that can be difficult to handle.

Don _____

Something that was particularly difficult for me was trying to build new memories. I had to make a conscious choice to celebrate holidays with my other children. I chose to try to make everything as normal as possible — when I didn't want to.

The first anniversary of Jacob's death was fast approaching, and we wanted to get away from the phones. We were sure people would be calling, and we would appreciate their thoughtfulness, but we didn't want to deal with, "How are you doing today?" Actually, we knew this would be a special time for us and we didn't particularly feel like sharing it with anyone else, so we decided to leave town for a few days.

Peggy _____

We had done a lot of traveling together as a family, but this would be the first trip since Jacob's death. We wanted to go where the five of us had never gone, where there would be no television, and where we would just have each other.

Before, we had a lot of special days—we celebrated anything we could. But the kids had said that "nothing's special anymore, Mom." The desire just had gone out of me.

Now the kids were excited because this would be our first new memory—but I didn't want to do it. I wanted to remember all the old memories. So it was a big, and difficult, step.

Don _____

I told Peggy and the boys that we would be flying.

"Where, Dad? Where are we going?"

"I'm not going to tell you. It's a surprise."

"Is it San Francisco? Should we take clothes for up there?"

I smiled and answered, "Plan to take clothing for all kinds of different places."

They were so sure it would be San Francisco that they planned where they were going and what they were going to do, and they packed for it.

On Sunday we went to church, then to a church picnic. That night we spent at the Hyatt Regency Hotel at the Los Angeles airport, on the boys' special floor, the one that requires you to have a card to get to it. The boys were still asking, "Where are we going, Dad?"

"Well, you guys just guess," I teased. Finally, I dropped them a hint. "I don't think we're going to San Francisco."

We had talked before about going to Mexico as a family, but it just didn't occur to them that we would do that now.

The next morning, though, when we boarded the airport van, I whispered into the driver's ear, "Take us to the Air Mexico terminal."

We passed Western, we passed PSA, and they were all still trying to figure out where we were going. We pulled up in front of the Mexican airline entrance, but they still didn't catch on. It wasn't until Peggy read the signs and looked at the flight schedules that they realized we were going to Puerto Villarta. And then they were really excited.

We had gone to Rosarita Beach the weekend or so before Jacob died. This time, we were going to a different place. We were going to do some of the same things again, but we also were starting over.

It was a special family time for all four of us. We laughed a lot; we played charades; we went horseback riding; we went walking—and we did a lot of talking. Peggy and I reaffirmed our love for each other and our love for the kids as well.

Deciding to take that trip was a tough choice to make, but we all benefited and grew greatly through it. Had we known what we would come home to, though, we probably wouldn't have gone.

While we were away, another family stayed in our home. One day their son picked up a dart. He threw it into the air and it landed in his eye—and he lost the sight in his eye. As soon as we returned, those parents dropped a large lawsuit upon us.

We were stunned, but we knew that as a family we would just have to hang in there. We made a conscious choice to handle it in as godly a manner as we could.

We had to put our grief aside—again—and again we had to choose not to let the situation destroy us.

Fortunately, some of our choices were not so heart-rending. One had to do with money. One night, just a few weeks after Jacob's death, Don called us into the bedroom. He said, "Sit down on the bed."

We sat.

Then he said, "We need to discuss what to do with the money that's been put into Jacob's memorial fund. One group in the church is trying to buy a car for Mr. Cunningham. You know, he does a lot of things for the Lord, and he really needs a car that will run. We could use some of the money for that. What do you think?"

We each took a turn and expressed how we felt and what we thought. I said, "That sounds like a good idea to me, but what do you boys think? Do you have any other suggestions?"

We discussed several positive things that the boys suggested, and no one was afraid to mention Jacob's name. I saw a great beauty in that. We all felt very comfortable during the conversation, and there was no hesitation about trying to determine just what Jacob would have done.

Little Donny said, "Well, I think we should give the money for the car. I think my brother wants us to do that."

Braxton said, "That's what Jacob would want, and because that's what he would want, that's what we want. We think you should do it, Dad."

We all agreed, and then we watched a television program together.

We made another choice about money later when someone suggested that a part of Jacob's memorial fund be applied toward a church building project, with the building being named after Jacob. To be honest, it was a temptation, because we knew that way everyone would remember our boy.

But Braxton and Donny objected. Whenever we had an opportunity to invest money in Jacob's name, we always asked, "What best represents Jacob? What are we trying to accomplish? Would Jacob be pleased with what we're doing?" And the boys always led the way. They continually helped us keep our priorities straight.

So this time Braxton said, "That wouldn't be what Jacob would want. He would want the money to be used for the kids. So why don't we do that rather than build a building?"

Braxton was right, so as a family, we chose to invest in a ministry for children. We all knew that would bring the greatest long-term benefit.

Don _____

There was another choice Peggy and I had to make that was hard to face. For months after the funeral, people would call, and the first question the caller would ask was, "How are you?"

That created quite a pressure because if we answered truthfully, "We're not doing well," they responded in a negative way, and we could tell they felt guilty. That wasn't what they wanted to hear.

If we said, "We're doing okay. We've had a good day," we were lying, but then they apparently felt free to pour out how bad they were feeling. We couldn't win. And it sometimes was hard to figure out who had lost the child.

We took it as long as we could, but I finally had to put a stop to it. So I reluctantly made the choice to speak out. The next call I got I said, "I appreciate the fact that you are calling, and seem interested, but it's very hard on us when you ask how we're doing." I explained what the responses had been – not only from him, but from nearly everyone who called. I was firm. In fact, I was blunt, but I tried to be kind at the same time. "I don't want you to do this any more. I really don't care much how you are feeling. That is not important to me right now."

Surprised, the caller said, "Don, what do you mean? We feel so bad. I wish you could understand how we are grieving . . . "

I answered, "We are dealing with our own grief now, and it isn't fair for you to call and put that kind of pressure on us."

"Well, you really can't blame me for what happened – and I'm just trying to help."

"We don't blame anybody, but we have to keep things in perspective. I realize you feel bad about Jacob being gone, but we walk by an empty room every day. We sit down to a table every night where there's an empty chair. You feel bad – but I'm devastated! You saw him once every month or two; we saw him every day. We're constantly aware of what's missing, and it's not fair for us to have to hear how much you miss him. We can't tell you how we really feel because it hurts you and it seems to intensify your feelings."

"I didn't mean any harm . . . "

"I know."

I don't think the callers realized that this was killing me. I wanted to tell them how much I hurt. The ability to share this deep hurt would be a long but rewarding process for me, but God was once again warming the room.

It was hard for all of us to understand what was going on, yet I believe it was one of the biggest areas of growth in all our lives. Through dealing with it and not letting it get the best of me, I learned not to be phony. I could not put on a show; I had to be real.

And the fear I had that others wouldn't understand was put aside. They did understand, and they honored my requests.

Understanding of the whole situation began to come to our boys, too, and sometimes it came in surprising ways.

14

The Boys Begin to Understand

"Mom! Jacob's back."

Early one morning about three weeks after Jacob died, Donny had come into our bedroom.

"No, honey, I'm sorry. Jacob's not back. He's gone to be with Jesus," I said quietly.

"No, Mom! No! I saw him. He's here! The angel brought him to me so I could see him. He's here!"

I knew what had happened. "Oh, Donny, you dreamed that. The angel brought Jacob to you in a dream. Isn't that exciting?"

In an explosion of anger, he screamed at me, "Jacob IS here! You just won't let me see him. He IS here! He IS!"

He began running through the house, calling him, trying to find him, then ran back into the bedroom, crying, "I have to go to the garage. He must be there."

Feeling helpless, I sighed, "No, Donny. Jacob is dead. He is gone and he is not coming back."

He was certain Jacob was there, and I was crushed — I didn't know how to explain through my own hurt that he wasn't. I couldn't accept it myself, how could I ever convince Donny?

I helped him get his shoes on, and as I tied the laces I broke down. Donny jumped up and headed for the garage, and I fell on my face. I cried out for the Lord to help me — I just didn't know what to do or what to say to Donny.

After he saw that Jacob wasn't there, and came back in, I realized I didn't need to explain. The Lord had come to him and helped him understand. And I knew that when Donny needed it again, the Lord would come to him again.

One evening several months later, during the Christmas season, we read about the time the angel appeared to Mary. Don asked the boys, "Have you ever known anyone who had an angel appear to them?"

"Yes, I did," Donny beamed.

Surprised, Don asked him, "When was that?"

He turned to me and said, "You remember, Mom. When you told me that Jacob was dead." His eyes grew large with wonder and he said, "But you know what, Mom? The angel came and told me Jacob was alive. And he is alive. He's in Heaven and he's alive."

Don _____

Another day, Donny asked, "Daddy, if Jacob is in Heaven, why is his body in the ground?"

That was a hard question for me, and I didn't know how to respond. Then before I could answer, he asked, "If Jesus loved him so much, why did He take my JJ away from me?"

I started to explain, "The Bible says . . . ," but decided on another approach. I found a kernel of corn and said, "Let's get a knife from the kitchen. I want to show you something." We cut the kernel open and looked at its outer shell.

"Do you see that little soft thing there inside the hard shell?" I asked. "That's the living part of the kernel. But before it can ever grow, the hard outside shell has to break open. Then the soft material can grow into a little stalk, a little stem, and then it will get bigger, and even bigger, until finally some ears of corn can grow on the stalk.

"That's what happened to Jacob. This hard outer shell is where the body is, but that's been opened up now and what was on the inside, his spirit, his soul, has been released. That's the growing part. That's the part that went to be with Jesus. So, even though his body is here, what was inside of Jacob that made him alive, that's gone to be with Jesus."

He looked up at me and back at the kernel. I could see the studying going on in his little mind. "But Jacob was in the casket."

"Yes, he was. And he was so cold and pale, so white. Do you remember that?"

"Yes, Daddy."

"Well, that's only the house Jacob lived in. Now he's not there anymore. He's not home. So it's not what it used to be. When we go to visit Jacob's grave, we're only going to the place where Jacob's house is. Jacob is with Jesus."

He seemed satisfied.

Peggy _____

Donny never did have much trouble expressing his feelings. One day we went into a store, and he suddenly sat down and began crying. "I hate it that my brother's dead! I hate it that my brother's dead!" he sobbed.

Sometimes he would dress in Jacob's clothes, or play a game with Jacob and hold conversations with him. He would ask Jacob questions. Several times when we were riding in the car, Donny asked Jacob, "Why did you ride your bicycle in the street?"

One evening we went to Marie Callendar's for dinner. The waitress happened to be a girl who had babysat for us at times. Curious, she asked, "Where's your other boy?"

Before anyone else could say anything, Donny looked her square in the eyes and declared quite loudly, "He's dead. He's gone. He's dead."

She stared in shock, and people all around us turned to look. The rest of us were stunned and really couldn't say anything other than, "Yes, he's gone."

"Oh, I didn't know," the waitress muttered uncomfortably and quickly left our table.

When Donny did these things we usually just let them pass. We never asked him to be quiet. Sometimes we cried, because he really just said what the rest of us were feeling.

He usually said or did these things at strange times, times when the rest of us were not thinking particularly about Jacob — when there was a lull in the conversation, or while we were eating. In a sense, it was as though the Lord allowed it to sink into each of us at a different level each time Donny said something. We would reflect on it in our own way, and it became more real for each of us every time.

Many times it seemed Donny needed no response. In a way, he clicked out; he was so intense in his little one-track mind, that he just said what he thought, and didn't expect anyone to answer.

One day Donny and I went to the grave with a girl-friend of mine. We stood there for a few minutes, and suddenly Donny grabbed her legs and put his head against her knees and cried, "My JJ's gone. I don't know why he went away. JJ's dead. My brother's dead."

She just rubbed his head and patted him.

I used to think sometimes that, as parents, we had to explain every detail to our children. But I don't believe that any more. God knows our pain and our confusion, and He helps our children understand, as well. Sometimes He speaks to them through other people, and sometimes through us, but sometimes it's simply through His own Holy Spirit. He just eases their minds and comforts their hearts.

Don

Braxton's reactions were much different from Donny's. Each boy responded out of his own personality type, and for the most part, as Donny spoke out, Braxton withdrew.

In fact, one of the earliest fears we had was that of losing two boys instead of just one. At the hospital the night of the accident, we saw Braxton's immediate, intense response, but then we saw him quickly close himself off and become quiet about his feelings.

Braxton suffered a great deal more pain than anyone realized. This boy lost his confidant, the one he shared most of his hours with. He lost the person he probably was closer to than any other. He lost the little brother he had been the protector of.

He also lost a lot of his own youth. Because he was brought to the core of life's realities so quickly, he was forced to accept things he didn't understand.

In addition, he felt betrayed. He was the first to see his injured brother after the accident, and then others told him, "Jacob is going to be okay." And he trusted them.

When he got to the hospital, he discovered that what they had said wasn't true, and he couldn't understand why they had deceived him. He couldn't put it into words, but his heart cried out, "Were they trying to protect me? From what? They said my brother would be okay, so I expected him to BE okay. They said he would be. They lied to me."

This sense of betrayal spilled over into another area as well. I saw Braxton as a young boy whose life was shattered because his best friend was gone — and his other friend, Jesus, had taken him.

I quickly became aware that he could very easily lose his relationship with God, because he had prayed and asked God to heal his brother. This realization — which coupled itself with a memory of mine — greatly alarmed me.

Instantly transported back to my childhood, I relived an experience we went through with my cousin Jimmy which had devastated me and, at that time, left me fearful of God. Jimmy and his younger brother Jackie, who was 15, were supposed to go somewhere together one evening, and Jimmy refused to go with Jackie.

While Jackie was walking home, he was hit by a drunken driver and killed. Jimmy was never the same afterward. He always felt he was to blame for his brother's death because he didn't go with him. If he had been along, he might have seen the car coming and been able to warn Jackie. Unfortunately, their father never was able to convince him that it wasn't his fault and that it wouldn't have made any difference — Jimmy couldn't have seen the car any quicker than Jackie did because Jackie was hit from behind.

Nobody could ever take the time to help Jimmy, and his life was a tragedy from that point on. It was partly because when somebody dies, that person seems to become a hero bigger than life. Nobody ever again said anything bad about Jackie. All they talked about were Jackie's good points, and Jimmy felt he could never measure up. It nearly destroyed him.

After Jacob's death, Jimmy called me. He knew how it could be and he wanted me to be very careful. He warned, "Don't let happen to Braxton what happened to me."

I knew I didn't want Braxton to suffer the same problems and hurt that Jimmy had endured, but I was walking into a new area and wasn't sure just how to handle it. I didn't know how many of Jimmy's problems were from outside sources and how many from inside himself. I don't think he knew either. And neither of us knew how my uncle could have lessened any of Jimmy's guilt. I don't know how you stop making somebody larger in death than they were in life, either. I guess it just goes with the territory.

When I saw Braxton on that same dangerous curve, though, I knew what was in the balance. Peggy and I had opportunities to console each other, and other people were sensitive to our needs. But few were sensitive to Braxton's needs—because "children bounce back." Yet I saw him losing his innocence, something he never would have again, and I saw him possibly losing his trust in God.

His devastation and his not knowing what to say or how to respond drove him to retreat into silence. I think it was particularly hard on him because he's naturally a reserved person. In fact, we didn't worry much about this quiet nine-year-old and his feelings, even at the funeral home. He responded to being in a place where quietness was expected, and we were comfortable with that.

We had enough to do dealing with Donny—he didn't understand the need for quiet. In retrospect, I'm sure Braxton experienced horrendous feelings, but he thought, *This is a quiet place, and I can talk with Mom and Dad later.* But later never came. Family came and went; people were in and out; we became exhausted and went home and to bed. The next day we prepared for the funeral, and then we were back at the quiet place again. Braxton just kind of got eaten up in the whole thing, and we were content to allow it.

But one day, a long time later, he said, "The thing I hated most about that funeral was that you got to say something, Daddy, and, Mama, you got to say something, but I didn't. And I wanted to get up and say something about my brother."

That shocked us.

It never occurred to us that Braxton would want to say anything at the funeral; he was just a little boy and we would have assumed he couldn't handle it. Now we realize we should have let him. That was his brother, and he wanted to express his loss. He felt he *was* capable of it.

We really regret that situation, and if we could go back and do it over, we would spend time alone with Braxton, and draw him out, and find out what he was feeling and what he wanted.

The first few days after the funeral, people included him in things so, heartsick as he was, he still didn't feel the loss as much as he did later on. As the weeks and months passed, he became more aware of what he really had lost, but he didn't want to talk about it. Added to his natural quietness was the fact that he realized Peggy and I would weep sometimes, and it was as though someone had said to him, "Don't talk to Mom and Daddy about Jacob, because they'll cry. If you just don't remind them, they'll be okay."

Sometimes Donny had nightmares during those trying months. One night Peggy took him into her arms and said, "Jesus will protect you." Braxton was standing behind her, and he blurted, "Sure, just like He protected Jacob."

That devastated us, but it made us realize how deeply Braxton really had been hurt by the whole thing.

As soon as we recognized what was going on with him, we tried to walk him through his feelings and relieve him of the pressure he was carrying. We began to be more open in our conversations about his brother. We tried not to ignore any situation, and we repeatedly assured him it was all right to cry. We explained that when Mommy and Daddy cried it wasn't always because we were hurting, but sometimes because we just missed Jacob, and that it was natural, and that he could cry too. We encouraged him to talk about what he was feeling, to try to put it into words.

About eight months after Jacob's death, a friend of ours who was a professional counselor offered his services free of charge. He had met with us right after Jacob died, and though at that time we seemed to be handling things pretty well, he knew hard times would come. He wanted us to know he was available whenever we needed him. Then he called from time to time in the months that followed to check on our well being.

When Peggy and I began praying for a friend for Braxton who would not see him as the pastor's son who was supposed to be "super-strong," or as a child who was too young to understand what had happened, we recognized Tom as an answer to that prayer. He knew what turbulence was going on underneath Braxton's calm surface and wanted to help him, or any of us, through that difficult time. Through Tom, God provided the special friend Braxton so desperately needed.

Tom's style of counseling, rather than asking you what you feel, is to get down next to you and do something with you, and just talk so that a friendship develops. He and Braxton played marbles together. Braxton felt comfortable with him and started to share his feelings. Tom helped him begin the process of opening up to someone outside the family. He listened to Braxton and constantly reassured him that his feelings weren't bad, that they were normal, and that he was doing a good job of dealing with them.

We noticed a change in Braxton after the first visit. He wasn't as tense. He was more open and more ready to talk. For the first two weeks after Jacob died, Braxton had been careful of what he said or how he said it, but after he began seeing Tom he became more like himself again, able to laugh and joke some and just be a kid.

He began expressing his personal feelings more, too. One day the four of us went to Palm Springs, and we took some James Dobson tapes on adolescence with us. We listened to them together, and talked. At one point, Braxton said, "Do you really want to know how *I* feel, not how I feel about Jacob?"

On our trip to Europe Braxton constantly said things to Donny like, "Stay over here by Mommy." Or to Peggy, "Mom, don't let him get by the curb—can't you walk on the other side?" He continually wanted to be the caretaker. We had to keep reminding him that Donny wasn't his responsibility, and that we were there, yet we sensed panic in him. Directed toward his brother, it came out as anger when Donny would drop three steps behind or walk two steps ahead.

We finally realized that Braxton's own feelings were separate, and sometimes quite different from what we expressed together as a family, and we were able to draw him out more and get him to talk more about them, at least within our family setting.

One thing that helped him through this tough time was the trip we took to Israel together, just Braxton and me, in November, about two months after Jacob died.

I knew a number of the other people who were going, but I wasn't concerned about them, just about Braxton and me spending time together, being able to talk and enjoy one another and building our friendship. I think he was looking forward to having Daddy to himself, not having to share me with anybody. His excitement about it showed—he talked about it all the time, and he could hardly wait, and he knew exactly what he wanted to do. He asked a lot of questions about what was going on over there, what he'd see, if he would see soldiers, and if he'd see where David slew Goliath. He wanted to know what we would be doing and if we would get to stay together.

One day when we had been there about seven days, we boarded a bus headed for Egypt and the Sinai Peninsula. The weather was sunny, hot and humid, and the air conditioner wasn't working. We stopped to pick up some security guards, and with them came the smell that is strictly their own. As we traveled we sang to break the monotony of the desert scenery. When we ended one particular song, Braxton got up and walked to the back of the bus.

After fifteen or twenty minutes, one of the men tapped me on the shoulder and said, "Maybe you ought to check on Braxton. He's been sitting in the back of the bus, staring out the window for quite a while."

I moved back and sat down with him. Tears were running down his cheeks. I put my arm around him and asked, "What's the matter, Son?"

"I was just thinking about Jacob," he choked.

"What were you thinking about?"

"About how much I miss . . . him and how much I'm going to miss him . . . and how I don't have anybody to take his place, and I'm never going to have a brother like that again . . . and I just don't know what to do . . . "

I put my arms around him. "It's natural to feel that way, honey," I comforted. "Daddy doesn't have any real good answers for you, either, because I don't know what's in store for you. But I know that, whatever it is, it is going to be good. We're going to make the best of this situation. We simply have to go through it a day at a time."

That's what I told him then, and that's what I continue to tell him now. It really is one day at a time. We can't look too many days ahead.

"I just feel so lonely," he murmured.

I answered him, "I know. You'll have to deal with Jacob's death each day as it comes. Some day it won't be as bad as it is today."

"It's so hard, Dad. I don't like feeling like this."

"I know, Son. But there is nothing wrong with what you feel. I appreciate that you trust me enough to tell me about it. That's important to me. You need to be able to express that, and you don't need to worry about how I feel. You just need to make sure I understand how you feel."

Then we hugged and held each other for a little while. I wondered if maybe this trip had been a mistake—the long bus ride would give him a great deal of free time to think.

Later, when Braxton was spending some time with someone else on the tour, I had a tough time of my own. Reflecting on what Braxton had said and how he had felt, I shifted gears in my mind and began talking to myself, and to God.

I became angry with Him and muttered little sarcastic remarks about His ability to provide. "Well, here we are, so many miles from where it all happened, and I tried to leave it all behind so we could build our relationship and enjoy ourselves, and You let all his memories come back. How come, God? Can't You just put this thing on the skids for two weeks and let that boy have a good time? Can't he just be a boy? After all, he hasn't done anything to You to have to go through such pain. Why does he have to carry the weight of this thing? And why does he have to feel so bad?"

Needless to say, for a little while there wasn't much response. My mind was not on spiritual things, and I got even more upset. "How come You can't provide for him right now and take away that pain? Why can't You ease the memory? Can't You let him put it out of his mind, and let these two weeks be a good break for him? Instead, he has to sit down and cry. It's not fair. He shouldn't have to go through this without some kind of release."

Finally I felt God's words begin to come into my heart as they had at Jacob's funeral: "I am the God of Jacob," and then He added, "and the God of Braxton, too." I didn't know if I could believe what I was hearing.

His words to me continued, "As I am the God of Jacob, I am the God of Braxton, and I know better than you what he needs and what needs to be done here. You need to trust Me, and you need to allow Me to do My work. And you need to believe that I am able to do that which I have said."

God's voice, though not audible, was nevertheless real to me, and the experience moved me. He said what my heart needed to hear. I remembered when, in Micah, He blared out to the people, "Wherein have I troubled you?" Now He asked me the question, "Okay, you're blaming Me for all this—now, wherein have I troubled you? What did I do?"

His voice came to me in a series of strong impressions. "You must trust Me. Even when you don't think I can do it, you still have to trust Me. Just jump out in faith and believe that I'm able to do what is necessary. I know the pain Braxton is going through far better than you, and not one arrow has pierced his soul that hasn't touched Me and hurt Me as well. I know what needs to be provided for him right now."

Gradually, I felt a deep, overall assurance that God really was in control. And I saw Him work in the days that followed.

The tour director had said to the others before we left on the tour, "We're going to be taking a nine-year-old boy with us—his brother has just been killed and he needs this trip. We don't normally take youngsters, but we are making an exception this time. His name is Braxton, and we're allowing him to come with his father."

So all the people were prepared ahead of time. As the days went by, they became involved in Braxton's loss and showed him a great deal of love and care. It soon became obvious that it was Braxton's group and that everybody else was merely a part of it.

When Braxton would get moody or just go off and stare into space, the people understood, and he felt their acceptance. They let him do things, and they made him feel special. Sometimes he cried, and they would take time out to make him feel, not just a part of a tour, but a part of a family.

Our guide, a lieutenant colonel in the Israeli army named Shagra ben Yosef, took Braxton under his wing. He spent time talking to him about how losing someone close to us hurts. "We have to be strong and go on," he counseled.

They spent a lot of time together, and he arranged for Braxton to drive the boat on the Sea of Galilee and hold a machine gun with Israeli soldiers on Masada. He understood Braxton's feelings. He told him how he fought in the wars of Israel and about how he had felt during those years when he lost friends and brothers who were close to him.

"You can't stop. You just have to go on. The strong get up and they keep going," he said.

Braxton told me some of what they talked about, and I saw his excitement about the wars Shagra had been in and what he had seen and done. I also saw his excitement about knowing somebody was concerned about him.

Shagra gave me bits and pieces of what they discussed. "You have a good boy," he encouraged. "Braxton understands far more than what you think a boy his age would understand. We've been able to talk."

On this trip, I saw God undergird Braxton with people who didn't need to be concerned, but who were. They knew they would see him for only a few days in their lives, and then probably never again, but they always let him know how much they enjoyed him. God provided him with a "grandmother" and with "aunts" and "uncles," and the trip became what I had hoped it would be, a special experience in Braxton's life.

I can still see the hurt in Braxton. I doubt it will ever go away, but it becomes different as time goes on. At first it was the sharp pain of a cut or wound, then through the process of healing, it turned into more of a dull ache. It doesn't hurt so much all the time now, but the pain is still there.

I think it will be eased a great deal when he is finally able to find a friend near his own age, a confidant he can trust himself with again. I believe his relationship with

Shagra was the beginning. That, and the time Braxton spent with Tom, have opened the way.

Another thing that has helped open the way to understanding and acceptance — for all of us — is the way God has brought answers to a number of our difficult questions.

15

Answers for Tough Questions

"Daddy, don't you know that I really hurt? Everybody seems to forget about *my* feelings."

When a traumatic event like the death of a child occurs, there are so many situations that must be dealt with, so many troubled emotions, and such chaotic changes taking place so quickly that most people simply cannot keep their thoughts straight. Everyone is affected so differently that it's hard to know just what is going on.

And many hard questions are asked. This one came from Braxton.

A few days after Jacob's death, a lot of people were at the house we had just moved into and, because the pain Peggy and I were experiencing was so visible, they centered their attention on us. When they looked at the boys, they didn't see so much suffering.

Donny was so outspoken about his that you knew whether he was hurting or not, and you could just go along with his reality. With Braxton, for a while people watched him to see how he would respond, and when he didn't break down and cry, in their minds they pronounced him fit and ready to resume a normal life. Yet it was Braxton who had seen his brother lying unconscious in the street. It was Braxton who had called his mother to tell her that Jacob had an accident. He took upon himself a great deal of the resulting pain and sorrow, and part of that load was not wanting us to hurt any more than we already did.

Another part was that, because people didn't really believe he was suffering, they didn't talk to him much. So he kept everything inside. After a while, as I sat on the couch, Braxton came over and crawled onto my lap. He sat there quietly for a few moments, and then, without moving, murmured just loud enough for me to hear, "Daddy, they don't seem to know that I hurt, too."

I read between his words and heard, "They're not letting me be a part of this." Realization of that truth jarred me, and I put my arm around my son and held him close.

A little while earlier, one of our men had said to Peggy, "Well, I wouldn't worry too much about the kids. They'll bounce back — they're resilient. They probably won't even remember as the years go by."

Another time, one of our young mothers said, "You're lucky Donny is so young. He won't remember this." In a way, I had hoped she was right. But I soon learned that children remember and feel much more than we suspect.

When Braxton came to me that day, I recognized that the adults were minimizing the boys' feelings. People were not aware of the relationship that Braxton and Jacob had enjoyed and thought it could be forgotten quite easily. Those outside our family just didn't realize how much time and energy and effort the boys had shared. Perhaps they were too far removed from the close relationship of brothers growing up together.

They knew that sometimes time does erase memory, and they really wanted to ease our minds, so they tried to give us advice. Unfortunately, it came in the form of pat answers. Adults often are satisfied with these, though, because they understand what is behind them. If you get somewhere close to the truth with an adult, the rest is usually fairly obvious and he can arrive at an acceptable conclusion himself.

But that doesn't work with children, and people really didn't know what to say to the boys. So they would try to dismiss them with comments like, "God will provide."

Or, "Don't you worry honey, Jesus is going to take care of you."

Even, "You should be thankful that Jacob's with Jesus right now."

All these things may be true, and they may be good, but they don't mean much to a nine-year-old kid. And they certainly don't help a three-year-old. Young boys don't understand those concepts. Kids are not concerned about Greek or Hebrew syntax, or theological answers to questions they are not asking. They just want to know, "How come my brother is dead?" and, "What does *dead* mean?"

Kids' questions are often simple, but at the same time they can be some of the most profound a person is asked. They make you stop and think about biblical truths. And the kids want answers that are simple enough for them to understand, something they can hold on to.

Peggy and I had been through hurts before—oh, nothing like this, of course—but our skin had been toughened a little. We knew we would rebound eventually; we knew we could survive—we had learned a little about how to help ourselves. But this kind of hurt is fresh and new to a child. He hasn't had enough other experiences to prepare him for it or to help him know how to handle it. Sure, they know other people who have died, but they weren't so close to home. Jacob's unexpected death had to be one of the most devastating things that could happen to our other boys—it was so final.

So that day, Braxton had no resources to fall back on. Realizing all this, I said to him, "Braxton, we're all going through this for the first time. Not just you and me, or Mommy and Donny, but all these other people, too. They want to help us, but none of us knows quite what to do for the other. I'm sure they know you're hurting, but they don't know how much, so we're just going to have to try to help strengthen each other now."

I hugged him even tighter and kissed him. I knew he would have to experience the hurt and I wanted to try to patch things up for him a bit with a good, clear answer. But how could I? I wasn't sure of the answer myself—and I was an adult.

I finally said, "You're right. Some other people don't really understand, but Mommy and I both know that you are hurting a lot. Your feelings for Jacob are strong and I know they are very real."

He accepted what I said, but he added, "Daddy, I just don't know what to do."

"Well, Brackie, we don't know either. We just have to take this one step at a time. We'll do what we have to do when we have to do it. But if you keep feeling that you're not getting enough attention, or that people don't understand, you come back to Daddy again and let's talk some more about it."

One family did understand and help, and a part of Braxton's answer came through them. They asked him to go to the beach with them. Another day they took him to a football game. As they included him in their activities, they made him feel that he had a place with them.

Also, I made a special effort to spend more time with him and try to encourage him. I wanted to be not only a good father for him, but a friend, too. Someone he could come to without fear, any time, and talk things over with. I tried to take up a little bit of the empty space that his brother had left.

I felt he needed that from me—Donny was too many years younger than Braxton to be able to fill any of that void. In fact, Peggy and I both pulled the boys much closer under our wings than we ever had before because, here in the new house, in this strange neighborhood, they just didn't have anyone else.

The question Braxton had asked needed an immediate answer, even if it was somewhat incomplete. He needed to know, right then, that I cared. So I had told him what I could.

Some of the other questions that came up could not be answered quite so quickly. One bothered me for a long, long time.

Just a couple of weeks before the accident I had made the statement in one of our evening services, "I don't know what I would do if anything were ever to happen to one of my family." I really felt my whole world would fall apart. I didn't think I could survive it.

But it did happen. And I did survive it. Yet not without a great deal of confusion and difficulty.

For some time after the accident I repeatedly asked myself, "Isn't it true that the steps of a good man are ordered of the Lord? And didn't God promise that He would uphold the righteous?" (Psalm 37:23 and 17).

"If so," I continued to ask, "where was Jesus when Jacob was hit? Where was He when my wife received word about the accident? How did He order our steps to put our boy in the ground?"

We quickly found ourselves in the midst of a severe storm in our lives. Yet I remember clearly that when the word first came, I was immediately possessed of an unexplainable calmness. To this day, I don't fully understand it, but I do know that the presence of that calm allowed me to face the storm, confident that we would come through it.

Some time later I remembered the evening Jesus instructed His disciples to get into a boat and go before Him to the other side of the Sea of Galilee (Matthew 14:22-33). As Peter and the other disciples loaded the boat and pushed off from the shore, I'm sure there were thoughts of what must lay before them. They remembered the miracles they had so recently witnessed—the blind receiving sight, the lame beginning to walk, the dumb speaking, even the dead being raised to life. Who could know what else was going to happen? Yes, this was going to be an exciting time.

Little did they suspect that before the next miracles would come, a severe storm would threaten their lives, their beliefs and their devotion.

Moving across the sea, they talked about the things that had just taken place on the shore. The crowd had been so large that no one disciple saw everything, so now they shared what they had seen. Can you imagine how the faith of each man grew as they related their experiences? With confidence soaring, they felt invincible as long as Jesus was with them. They couldn't be beaten!

While they talked, one of them spoke a warning, "Look! Black clouds coming."

Another said, "They'll be on us in just a few minutes."

The wind suddenly became stronger, but these seasoned fishermen were not afraid.

A third man said, "We've handled many a storm worse than this. Remember that one last year? It was a rough one, but we beat it, didn't we?"

Confident of their abilities, they prepared themselves and the boat to weather this one as well. Besides, weren't they on a divine mission? And weren't they followers of the Master, Himself? Tragedy could never strike them. If anything were to threaten them, they could just speak the words and the elements would have to respond.

Soon, however, the wind became wild. Jagged lightning ripped across the sky, thunder crashed, and rain nearly blinded them. They became aware that this storm was much more severe than any they had ever faced before. Would they be able to meet the challenge? Was their faith strong enough to see them through?

Can you imagine them, taking turns, trying to quell the storm? First, Peter steps up, raises his hands and commands, "Peace. Be still." He steps back, fully expecting the storm to abate. Instead, the wind howls louder, the waves become bigger, and the thunder crashes with even greater force.

Then John tries, but with the same result. Each man takes his turn, but the storm continues to worsen and batters their boat unmercifully. Their emotions run the gamut from the victories of the previous meetings to shattered self-sufficiency. Their faith is crushed. In their secret hearts they each have thoughts like, *What will people think if we — the disciples of Jesus — end up at the bottom of the sea? We're doing what Jesus told us to — how can we sink in this storm? We have obeyed Him, but what will become of us now? Where is Jesus? Why isn't He here with us? Why isn't He protecting us?*

All those questions. No answers. The worst part of it was that Jesus had told them to go to the other side, and now He wasn't with them in their time of crisis. They were sure they would perish.

Were they really alone? Had He actually abandoned them? No. In the midst of their crisis, when things looked the blackest, He came to them, in a miraculous way, walking on the water.

The disciples had been no more alone than Peggy, Braxton, Donny or I was when we learned of Jacob's accident. We were never alone in our tragedy — it just took us some time to realize it. He is always in our situations, but so often He must wait for us to open our eyes to His presence.

The disciples were so consumed with their problems that they didn't see Jesus. Then suddenly, while the others screamed, "We're going down!" Peter saw a figure coming toward them out of the blackness.

"Look!" he yelled. "Do you see what I see?"

A new fear gripped the heart of each man as he looked in the direction Peter was pointing. What — or who? — could it possibly be?

Trembling almost beyond control, Peter called out, "Lord, is it You?"

"It is I," the familiar voice responded.

Impetuously, Peter cried, "If it is You, Lord, bid me come to You on the water."

"Come," Jesus said simply.

Peter stepped out boldly, in faith, in the midst of the biggest crisis of his life. He trusted the words of his Savior.

I have pondered this event often, and realize that at the moment Peter stepped out of the boat, he was not depending on himself, or on his spirituality — whatever the others may have perceived that spirituality to be. He depended totally on Jesus to see him through.

Of course, as we all know, midway through his walk of dependence, Peter took his eyes off Jesus. He may have thought, *Ah, now I've got the hang of this walking on water.* Or, more probably, he suddenly realized, *Hey! I'm in the middle of a storm! What am I doing out here on the water? I must be crazy!* At any rate, he began to sink.

Fortunately for him, he had the presence of mind to do what we are now learning to do. He called out to Jesus, "Lord! Save me!" With that call, he admitted his failure, and acknowledged his need for divine help. Jesus, always faithful to meet a need, immediately reached out and took Peter's hand, and pulled him out of the water.

I can empathize with Peter. Having seen a miracle performed in your life, there is no worse feeling than having it begin to evaporate before your very eyes because you forgot who had performed it. You learn very quickly to cry out, "Lord, save me." Not colorful words, but words that get the job done.

My family faced our storm, and we feared for our existence, too, as the disciples had. Yet comfort had come to my heart even before I really knew that Jacob was dead. My little boy himself, the soft, pliable meat of that little grain of wheat set free on the pavement of a road in San Diego, helped to open my eyes. I saw Jesus walking toward us to calm the threatening storm. Our hearts became receptive, allowing Jesus to have His way in the situation.

I was the pastor of a church; my family had been exposed constantly to spiritual truth and we were living as closely to that truth as we knew how; yet we were not sheltered from the storms of life. We were, in fact, normal people, with the same doubts and fears others would have and the same questions anyone else would ask. With the first notice of Jacob's accident, we wondered how we would respond to this situation and to the many people who were involved. The first assault of the storm, the accident itself, in a sense was the easiest part. The real onslaught came in the days to follow.

Yet, as we stepped from our boat onto the troubled waters, we became, in a way, oblivious to the things happening around us. Some thought we were in shock, but we just began living the experience in the grace and comfort of our Lord Jesus Christ. In Jacob's death, we learned to become more dependent on the hand of our Lord as He bade us come to Him. It was the point in our lives, and in our relationship as a family, where we stopped living and allowed Him to live in and through us.

One of the men who assisted me in performing Jacob's funeral service said, "We have all marveled at your faith, your strength and your courage." It took me a *long* time to realize that the way we responded was not ours at all. It was Jesus calming the storm in our lives. He revealed it to me little by little, and I am still learning.

Peggy _____

Probably the question we have asked ourselves more than any other, and still do, is, "How can we best help our boys deal with this and not be embittered for life from it?"

With Donny it wasn't so difficult because he spoke out his feelings freely whenever he had them. As we mentioned before, most of the time he didn't even really require any response from us—he just said it the way it was with him, and that was it.

With Braxton, though, it has been totally different. Because he kept most of his anger and frustrations inside, he became sullen and moody. From time to time we could see his rage building up and then he would suddenly explode.

Recently, in fact, he had become cold toward us and uncommunicative. We didn't know what he was thinking but sensed a rebellion. Yet we believed that he felt safe with us and secure in our love, enough to trust us to dig into his feelings and help him express what he couldn't say by himself. But we didn't press because we weren't sure just what the underlying cause was and actually were afraid that whatever we did might be wrong.

Things went along this way for a while, and then one day I got a phone call. "Mrs. Gregg," Braxton's school counselor said, "could you come to the school? Braxton has had a problem and we need to talk."

When I got there and saw Braxton I was shocked. He had shaved the sides of his head, and given himself a Bryan Bosworth haircut. (Bryan Bosworth was a University of Oklahoma linebacker.) I was disappointed and more than a little angry with Braxton. At the same time, I didn't want to be too tough on him because he really had been having a bad time of it.

A few years ago we probably would have let an incident like that pass by. But this time I called Don and we made arrangements to get away as a family again. We went to Palm Springs for two days and had one of the best times we ever had. We did begin to dig into Braxton's inner thoughts and were able to focus on his own reality instead of just the family's.

Since then we've been more able to remember that we are dealing with good boys — boys who love the Lord. We've tried to be more understanding of them because one thing we definitely want is for them to be able to express freely how they feel. It would be wrong for us to tell them that and then to clamp down on them when they get angry or depressed. That would tell them that we were only talking and didn't really mean what we said. Actually, there have been times when I've felt the same frustrations

Braxton felt and wanted to do some of the same things he has done, but I'm too old for that. Sometimes, though, I think it might have been good for me. Anyway, I don't begrudge him his chances any more.

Don _____

The day before the funeral Braxton asked me what was probably the toughest question of all: "Why did you do it?"

We had been playing catch and had sat down on the porch to rest a minute. In my effort to try to make him feel included in what was going on, I asked him, "Is there anything you want to know? Any questions you want to ask? If so, I want you to feel free to ask them."

He looked up at me, long and hard, and finally asked, "Daddy, how come you decided so fast to take Jacob off that life-support system?" It was too big a question—he couldn't ask it by itself—so several other questions came with it. "How come? Would Jacob still be alive? Was that machine keeping him alive? Would it keep him alive for a long time? How does it work?" And then the big one again, "How come you decided to turn off the machine?"

A child wants specific answers, and if he is really confused, he will keep asking you until he gets them. I had a hard time with his question, because I didn't have the specifics. Peggy and I knew in general why we did it, so I tried to explain. "Well, the doctor said there was no hope, and that in a few hours the swelling would increase so much that all the blood would be cut off from his brain and he would be dead. Then they wouldn't be able to use any of his organs for anyone else."

Braxton wanted to know, "Why didn't you wait for the two or three hours for a chance for a miracle? You've told us about miracles happening for other people. Why didn't you give Jacob a chance?"

Calmly I explained, "In theory, he was already dead. After two or three hours we would have to do it anyway."

But that wasn't what he was asking. He wanted to know, "Why did you do it?"

By this time I could hardly talk. I was crying. I really couldn't answer him because I didn't know myself why we had done it. In my mind I saw us all back there in the hospital room, where a trauma team was working, where donor doctors and transplant doctors were waiting, and where there were desperate needs all around. We had to see the big picture — of which we were just a small part — and we had to make the decision then.

Sitting on the porch, I felt the still-fresh pain even more deeply as I thought of the one child who was considered dead and the other who was now asking, "Did you maybe make that decision too quick?" And the pain made me begin to question what we did.

I didn't respond well to Braxton's question — it was so straightforward, and we were not used to that. Nobody asked us straightforward questions. They asked, "How are you doing?" or "Are you doing okay?" What is okay? What does "How are you doing" mean? Those are so non-specific that you can answer a lot of them without ever telling anybody anything about how you really feel. And, usually, the people who are asking don't really want to know anyway.

So I sat back and tried to tell Braxton what I could. I don't know if I answered his question that day or not. He wanted a simple answer, and all I had were complex explanations.

Just recently, several years later now, he asked me, "Do you have any regrets?"

Believe it or not, the question still gnaws at me. I'm still trying to figure out, Why did we do that? My answer was still pretty general. "Mommy and Daddy were forced to make some quick decisions that were very difficult, based upon limited knowledge we had at the time, and upon what the doctors told us, and upon the needs we saw and what we felt in the room. If we had delayed, Jacob's organs could have suffered damage and then we wouldn't be able to donate them to anyone. In a sense, Mommy and Daddy feel like Jacob's still alive because his organs are working in the bodies of other people. They have a little piece of Jacob with them. That's the way we looked at it. We didn't have a lot of time to think it through, but we feel like we made the right decision. There really was no question about waiting – we weren't given that option."

He thought about what I said; he could see it still wasn't easy for me to talk about it.

"Daddy, that must have been very hard."

"Yes, it was. It was probably the hardest thing Mommy and Daddy ever had to do, or ever will have to do – but we don't regret it."

He responded softly, "I love you, Daddy, and I love Mommy," and he hugged me.

16

Handling Anger With Honesty

Peggy _____

The doctor said to me, "Don't come back until you go through your anger."

Shocked, I replied, "But I'm not really angry. I'm just so depressed."

Kindly, he explained, "It's especially hard for Christians to go through anger because they feel it's wrong. They think they should not be angry. When they are, they try to deny it. They suppress it, and then they don't understand why they feel so rotten."

He reminded me that depression is anger turned inward, either not admitted or not expressed. Then he added, "If you continue to deny it, if you don't allow yourself to feel it, you will make yourself physically ill."

I really didn't understand why I felt so down because this was the third year after the accident, and I thought I should be myself again by now.

I seemed to spend the first year trying to believe that what happened really did happen. It was so unreal. Every morning I woke up with a knot in my stomach. Sometimes I had nightmares, dreaming that we had buried Jacob alive, that he wasn't really dead, that the doctors had made a mistake.

I experienced extreme insecurity because everything I thought I knew was yanked out from under me like a rug. The only thing I was sure of during that time was that God did exist. But I wondered, "Where did Jacob *really* go? He only made one little mistake with that bike. Or did the woman who was driving the car make the mistake? Was it a combination? Does God actually work like that?"

It had been easy to put the kids into God's hands and trust Him with them before, but after the accident I wondered, "Just what did I trust God for? I was willing to give all, but now that Jacob has gone with God, it's *all* of him, and I'm *not* willing. I didn't expect anything like this." Questions constantly invaded my mind.

Then about the second year acceptance began to come. And with it the deepening of the pain, and desperately missing Jacob. It took nearly the whole year for me to learn to live with that. When the third year began, I thought I had begun trusting God to eventually provide the healing I longed for. But that's when the anger began, all of a sudden. It overflowed me like a flood, and I could not control it.

People had told me I would experience anger, but I hadn't believed them. I thought it wasn't necessary for Christians to suffer anger. But the pressures kept mounting and the depression kept deepening. When I went to see the doctor, he finally made me realize what was happening.

However, I felt powerless to change it. I tried to put on a decently happy face, but fury tore at me from the inside and I felt trapped. It wasn't long before those inner feelings began to spill out into every area of my life. I was frustrated constantly. I couldn't pray through it or release it, no matter how I tried. A dark cloud, a feeling I never had before, greeted me every morning and hung over me the entire day.

Poor Don—I took a lot of it out on him. He couldn't do anything right; he didn't protect me enough; he didn't protect the boys enough. I was mad at him all the time. The boys were the only ones I could tolerate at all, and it surprised me, but I even became short with them.

As the holiday season approached that year, my anger began coming out at other people. Our church planned a Thanksgiving dinner for underprivileged people, to be served on a Sunday at a downtown hall. I couldn't find out how I was to prepare the turkey, whether I was to cook it at the hall or cook it at home; was I to cut it up, or bring it whole?

So I finally said, "Fine. Just fine. I just won't go at all."

That was so unlike what I would normally do.

When morning came, I was emotionally exhausted from the fight, and still angry. Then one of my closest friends called and asked, "Are you going to the church?"

To me her words were sparks, and they ignited the embers of my anger. Why did she need to know? Why did I have to tell her whether I was going to the church or not that morning? Those who were serving the dinner weren't going to church that day, but what business was that of hers? I remember saying to her, "Why do you ask?"

"I just wondered if you were going to drop your children off for church."

"No, I am not going to drop off the children," I barked. They had gone with Don earlier, but that still was none of her business.

"Oo-o-h, I can tell we're a little testy today," she teased. "I just thought maybe, if you were, you could pick some people up when you got there."

"It is just amazing to me that I have to be in charge of getting everyone everywhere!" I didn't know I could be so sarcastic.

"Does that mean you're not going to pick them up?"

"That's what it would mean under normal circumstances, but, because I'm the pastor's wife, I guess it doesn't mean that. It just means that I'm to go anyway, whether I want to or not!"

So I went.

Later, after this period of my life, I remember telling my girlfriend that I had fed my anger that entire day because she didn't call me back and ask what was wrong, what was going on with me that made me respond in a way she knew wasn't normal. I felt she should have called and yet I didn't know what I would have said if she had. Inside, though, I desperately wished she would.

During those months I was particularly angry at myself for saying the things I did, and for allowing people to see me like that. That wasn't really who I was, and it served to compound my anger.

In fact, I looked back on each time I had dedicated my children to the Lord, and scolded myself with, "What did you think you were doing when you gave them to God? You were allowing Him to do exactly what He needed to do in their lives." I couldn't imagine what I had been thinking at the time, and demanded, "Didn't you realize that this very thing was possible?"

I knew that the Scriptures say that it is appointed unto us once to die and after that the judgment. Nowhere are we promised that just because we are good Christian people and have done the right things will we be exempt from death. The truth is, it's going to happen to all of us. So I hauled myself over the coals with, "How could you have been so silly as to think your children could be protected from death just because you handed them over to the Lord?"

My increasing lack of control over what was coming out of me scared me. I'm sure it scared Don some as well because I didn't want any part of anything. I wanted to be left alone. I really wished I could go to a deserted island and just stay there until this thing passed.

Sometimes in a case like this people get angry with God. I didn't. Maybe I had been trained not to be angry with Him so I denied it, I don't know. The only anger I felt toward Him was for not helping me control this terrible, fierce, inner rage. He could have lifted some of the pressure, but He didn't. Yet I couldn't explain the pressure. I was never quite sure what I wanted Him to do.

One pressure I recognized was the feeling of having to mask my anger at church. I wouldn't allow myself to express it there.

Another stress was having to be with people in other places when I knew what my mood was.

I felt totally worthless, and didn't think I could live as angry as I was. I was damaging everything around me.

For months I had been struggling to hang on to a thread of sanity. I felt I had the choice of hanging on or letting go. I knew that if I chose to let go, I would be responsible for how I acted and what I did. So each day I consciously made a choice to hang on for a little longer.

Yet I also knew that if I were to let go and allow myself to become insane, I couldn't be responsible or accountable because I wouldn't be in control. It almost looked appealing, like a way out. These thoughts reflect the confusion I was living in.

On New Year's Eve we had a watchnight service. It had been just another angry day for me—nothing had gone right. I stood in the service praying, and the more I prayed, the more I became overwhelmed with the burden of it all. For the first time in my life I truly felt like giving up. I told the Lord, "There is just not one more day I can live in this anger. You will have to take it away. I cannot hold on any longer. This is it. I'm giving up."

I felt the Spirit of the Lord tell me, "You need to ask someone to pray with you."

I didn't want to do that—to admit to anyone that I was really angry. I had been trying for a whole year to hide it so how in the world could I share it with someone now and get them to believe the intensity of my need?

I felt the Lord saying, "But I want you to share it with someone."

In my heart I answered, "Lord, I don't have any idea who to go to."

He laid on my heart a certain person, and I said, "I don't want to go to her with this." I paused, waiting for Him to put someone else on my heart, but He didn't. So I went on, "All right. I'm so desperate, I'll go to her. But You are really going to have to meet me there because I simply can't."

So I went to this person and said, "Would you pray with me? I just have such a spirit of anger."

I wanted to explain, though I didn't understand it myself, but before I could say anything more, she said, "Let's just pray." She didn't need any explanation.

She began to pray with me. Finally she said, "You are releasing a lot of hurt, and the Lord is meeting you here, right now. He is taking it all away."

Instantly, instantly, I felt so relieved, so good inside.

I am not a person who gets depressed or stays angry. I can be really mad at a person one minute and the next minute not remember what I was angry about. So the depression after Jacob's death and the anger for that length of time was new and terrifying to me. Now, suddenly, wonderfully, I didn't feel it at all — for the first time in at least a year.

The relief was so great, and it was such a turnaround, that I was afraid it would all come back on me the next morning when I woke up. But it wasn't there at all. I continued to be frightened for at least three weeks. Every morning when I opened my eyes, I said, "Lord, don't let it be here today. I couldn't stand it." And it wasn't. It never came back. God had met yet another need, and in such a thrilling, spectacular way!

Don _____

I believe part of Peggy's frustrations grew out of the circumstances we faced through that whole three years. It wasn't a matter of dealing with just one situation. Before long we felt we had been thrown right into the midst of a real tangle.

Neither of us blamed God particularly, but soon after Jacob's death, it seemed everything else went wrong, too. We were involved repeatedly with insurance companies, and it seemed nobody was interested in dealing right with us. We found bills from doctors for hearing and speech therapy — when Jacob had been in a deep coma and had never come out. Some bills came so quickly we were stunned; others didn't come for many months and when they did we were shocked again. We knew some of those doctors had never seen Jacob — they were just on call. And we were expected to pay for that.

Then we were slapped with a lawsuit by someone we did a favor for by letting them stay in our home, and then their boy got hurt—and our insurance company had to settle that. The boy's father called Peggy one day and, since we were trying to be realistic and fair about the lawsuit, she assured him that we understood. He responded with, "Well, I know you understand because it's the same type of deal as with your son."

That hurt her deeply. Here is a man who goes home and talks to his son every day and still enjoys him, and will for who knows how long?—and he thinks his deal is like ours. Of course, it wasn't anywhere near the same, and his lack of compassion simply crushed Peggy.

Another painful frustration came to her when a woman said, "I know that to lose a child is high on the scale of stress, but it's nothing like losing a husband. At least you had your husband to help you through the grieving."

Many times she wanted to scream out at people, "You are not hearing me! You don't understand! I'm devastated!" A lot of people were caring, but Peggy just was not able to verbalize what she really felt. She couldn't seem to make anyone understand her pain.

It was only through finally being totally honest with God that she was able to find relief. If He is going to do anything in your life, He first must have you be honest with Him. We have to come to the place where we can tell Him about our deepest inner feelings, those we are most afraid to face or express. We have to let Him see that we really are fearful, angry, frustrated and doubtful.

This is one of the most widespread problems people have. As a pastor, when I counsel with individuals or couples, I find that the biggest hurdle they meet in handling their problems is the inability to be honest with God. They are extremely concerned about what others may think, but most of all they are afraid they will offend God.

So they go their way, covering their anxieties by saying, "God knows all about it, and if He wants to do something, He can."

One of the main problems we ourselves had to work through was the frustration we felt toward God's apparent inability to protect us. When we had done the very best we could, and had committed the children into God's hands, then we were angry because He "didn't do a very good job of protecting them." We accused Him of all sorts of neglect.

We said, "We could have kept them up here at home that week if God had just given us a warning sign that something might happen." But He didn't.

We said, "You know, God, it wouldn't have been this way if You had just done what You were supposed to do. It wouldn't have happened if . . . "

We said, "We don't like being placed in this position, and we don't think it's fair."

Because our family members were involved, it put all of our relationships in serious jeopardy. We let the kids go stay with my mother and father. My mother and father then let the kids go and stay with my brother and sister-in-law. The accident happened at my brother's house. The others all felt tension about how we would respond to them, and we had fears about it as well.

The lady who hit Jacob went to my uncle's church. And the question came up, "How will this affect the church?" There's no question but that the decisions that had to be made could affect the overall outcome for eternity for a lot of people.

Because of all these things, we had to struggle to walk the fine line that would keep our family relationships intact.

We had a lot of different feelings to sort out, and the only thing we could do was just be honest with God. We discovered that He is not offended by even our most intense feelings, no matter what they are. As our realization of that grew, so did our trust in Him.

He never does put His hand on our throat when we ask Him questions, so the more we went to Him, the more we learned to depend on Him.

When we were out on a limb with nowhere else to go, and we were still frustrated, and still had doubts, all we could say was, "There's nothing I can do with it, God. I just have to leap out in faith. I am totally dependent on You. I can't handle it myself."

We learned to trust Him.

Another thing we have learned is that it is necessary to verbalize our feelings. In order to be totally honest with God, you must first know what your feelings are yourself. So many times we aren't sure in our minds just what we are feeling, but when we have to put them into words, we are pressed to identify them. Then that clarifies them for us and we can begin to be honest with God about them. Until that time, it's too easy to assume that those vague, shapeless feelings will just go away by themselves. They won't. They get buried, and then come out later in ways that we don't recognize. If we can get our feelings out, we can deal with them and we can regain control.

Honesty with God also includes dual communication. We communicate with Him in prayer, in the same way as what we used to call a "rap session." When a person begins to pray, though, so many times he will say, "Now You speak to me, Lord, and tell me what I want to know." Or he will say, "Lord, I want You to just listen while I do all the talking." One or the other is expected to listen. When that is the case, though, there is no real sharing, no getting in touch with each other's heartbeat.

With Peggy and me, the main early communication — with each other, with the boys, and then with God — was about why it happened. Why didn't it happen to someone else's child? What did we do wrong? Did we make decisions prematurely? What could we have expected from the life-support system?

During those very painful months, we came to God over and over to ask, "Why did we make that decision? We felt You were leading us." We would see an item in the paper where someone's child had been in an accident and had some brain damage, or was in a coma for a while and then came out and was able to get well, and we would wonder, *Did we move too quickly?*

Without being able to verbalize our feelings to God, we would have continued to carry the fear, the doubt, and the anger and resentment that built up inside about trusting God to lead us in making the right decision, then wondering if we did. By verbalizing these things to each other and to God we had a calmness that we could not have had any other way. We were walking in the midst of a vicious storm, and He was there with us. We know because we talked with Him all along, and He responded.

One thing we must remember about anger is that it has to be directed in order to be resolved. Unresolved anger becomes counterproductive. It eats away at you. Eventually, a time will come when common sense wants to come in and you begin to realize your anger needs to be clarified and directed. When that time comes, you make a choice. If you begin directing it, you can, with the Lord's help, deal with it and resolve it. If you don't direct it properly, you become one of those people who walk around angry with everyone. They feel that everyone is after them, or that everyone wants to do them wrong.

Peggy and I have learned that whenever a church has problems, a lot of unresolved anger is present. People have feelings toward one another that you can't confront or bring out into the open because you will only make the situation worse.

I began to realize that my anger wasn't aimed at the lady who hit Jacob. Nor was it directed toward my family who were watching him. Sometimes it was directed at Jacob. Then gradually it became more and more directed at God. He soon let me know that His shoulders were broad enough to bear whatever I laid on Him. Once I reached the point where I could be honest with Him about my anger, He began working with me to resolve it.

God wants to help each of us resolve our hurts, but we must do our part. We all assume God knows how we are feeling because He knows everything—and that is true. But part of dealing with our hurt and anger is allowing God to experience them with us. When we do, He sort of kicks us out of neutral and into drive, and the Holy Spirit takes control and begins to show us that He is able to do what He says He will do.

This cannot happen, though, until we're honest with Him, until we can express to Him what we are really feeling. I think that is a breakthrough in any relationship. It's not that we are being disrespectful—we are just hurting. The Bible says: "Come unto me all you who are heavy laden and I will give you rest." We have to admit to ourselves that we are heavy laden, and then we have to let God know it. We don't usually do that until we cry out, "I can't handle it anymore."

I was angry at being placed in the situation where so many problems arose and so many relationships were at stake. It became important to me to be able to go directly to God and express how I felt. There was no way I could raise my arms and say, "Praise God that Jacob went home to be with Him."

That wasn't how I felt then, and it's not how I feel now. What I did say was, "I need some spiritual sight, God, because I need to see Your hand in all this. Otherwise, I am going to have a very difficult time, indeed."

I admitted to Him that for me to understand or accept Jacob's going, or see any purpose for it, I would have to see the fruit it would bring. If I couldn't see the fruit, I wouldn't be able to accept my son's death.

I also confessed, "I'm not the kind of person who can forget easily. I can forgive, but I don't know if a person can forgive without forgetting. I struggle with that."

God was fair with me. "You will have victory over Jacob's death, a day at a time," He promised. "Tomorrow there will be victory for you if you want it and if you need it. When you struggle, there will be something there to help you."

He has never failed me. There are days when it's more difficult than others, but today I have victory. Tomorrow I may not, but I know it is available.

One of the lessons I learned in this process is how the Holy Spirit helps us understand by drawing different points of reference from the Old Testament about how God deals with His people. This encouraged me because it showed me my thought processes were not all wrong.

In the book of Micah, for example, when the children of Israel complained, God asked them to come together. Then He said, "If I've wronged you, let Me know and I'll make it right. But let's come together and sit down and talk about it. You let Me know how you're feeling, and I'll fix it."

In Isaiah He said, "Come, let's reason together. Let's sit down at the table and tell each other how we're feeling."

It's like two opposing groups trying to come up with a solution to a problem, but with neither side understanding the other.

Or it's as though you say, "God, I gave you my life."

And God says, "Then give it to Me and trust Me."

Then when something happens you tell Him, "I feel You didn't do very well with what I gave you."

He then says, "What more could I have done? I've surrounded you with people."

You say, "Yes, but what are people when I lost my son? Those people don't mean to me what my son does. They're not as intimate with me as my child was." You're trying to come to God and express yourself.

God sits back and listens, allowing you the opportunity to ventilate on Him. Then He says, "But I'll show you how those people are important and I'll show you how this thing can work out. You're going to have to trust Me with it and you're going to have to walk with Me step by step. If you'll do that, I'll show you what the benefits will be. It's your choice. I've heard you, and My answer is, let's walk together and experience this together."

I really believe God experiences things new with His children each day. Otherwise it could be that when you get hurt, God would respond with, "Yes, all My kids get hurt." But He goes through each of these things with us because we are individuals. He corrects us when we get out of line. When we cry we see His heart because He cries with us. He hugs us when we need to be hugged. He pats us on the back when we need to be patted. Through our honesty, and being able to express our feelings, we don't fear Him.

Sometimes you get angry enough to say things you don't really mean. In most relationships that does permanent damage, but with God it doesn't. As a family we sensed that. We sensed that He was able to throw up some shields for us because He knew what the pain was like.

It would have been difficult if Peggy and I and the boys had not been able to come directly to God and share our true feelings and ask our questions. We were fortunate to have a source to go to, someone who was in complete control of everything that happened. We were able to bypass any middleman, and go right to the supervisor. He was able to bring the results we needed in our lives.

We feel that one of the most important things God wants us to share with others is the fact that we were not able to do anything for ourselves, and whatever was done, God did.

So many times we went to Him with our doubts and frustrations, and said, "God, You're going to have to show us that You really do care because, right now, we don't have anything else." And He did show us, in so many ways. He taught us that He can be trusted with our honesty, and this became part of the growing process in our lives. It has strengthened our trust in all His attributes, and has beautifully deepened our relationship with Him.

Our trust in Him also gave us the courage to face the various stages of grief honestly, though we really didn't know quite what to expect.

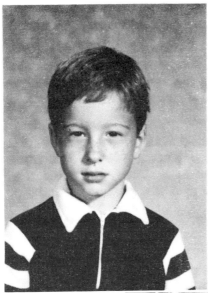

Jacob at kindergarten age.

Jacob always had a ball in one hand and a glove in the other.

17

The Ways of Grief

One thing I have learned by watching people through the years is that every individual handles grief differently. It is a mistake to predict just how a person will feel grief or how he will express it. Sometimes we think the person who cries the most loves the most, but it can be just the opposite. The other person may be every bit as intense in his feelings but not as able to express it. Yet there is no difference in the love or the depth of hurt; it's just that pain levels are different at different times.

Jacob was a special child to me because he needed me, seemingly more than the others did. He always wanted to be with me, and he liked the same things I liked. He looked like me, and he loved baseball as much as I did. When I was a boy my brother and I played catch a couple of hours every day, and I looked forward to doing that with my children. Jacob began to grow, and before long he'd grab a glove and have me working out with him. It was almost like reliving my childhood—as though I were watching myself grow up. Then he was gone—my childhood was suddenly and completely wiped out, and the only thing left was pain.

Peggy and I each felt the pain because of different things. I lost a playmate, my alter-ego. Peggy lost her little boy, the one she had spent so much time with, loving him and teaching him. Our feelings of loss were at opposite ends of the spectrum. We were both Jacob's parents, yet our relationship with him was so different. She missed reading bedtime stories to him. I missed the baseball.

We felt the pain in different ways, too, and there was no way we could compare it realistically, no way either of us could be sure that "it hurts me more than it does you"; or, "I love Jacob more than you do."

Yet I felt at times that we were in competition as to who hurt the most. If one of us would say, "I really miss Jacob this afternoon," the other would respond with, "You think *you* miss him. I did this or this today, and that was something he and I always did together." So many times I just didn't understand. The statistic someone gave us the night Jacob died, the one that said *in 75 to 80 percent of families where a child dies, eventually the parents end up getting a divorce,* stuck in the back of my mind. I couldn't forget that maybe we would be a statistic, especially during those quiet moments when neither of us knew what the other was thinking or feeling.

It was rocky at first because we each needed different kinds of responses. We needed to be talked to, or hugged, or reassured, or we just needed to be left alone. Many times as I sat in the front room, or at the kitchen table, I would steal a glance at Peggy and ask myself, "What does she need?"

Sometimes you can kick each other in the seat of the pants and get yourselves going, and it's just the right thing to do. At other times that could cause a great deal of damage simply because you don't know what the other person needs.

It was hard for either of us to express our needs because so much of the time we weren't even sure ourselves what they were. Through the years, though, we've each come to the point of asking what the other needs. Often, it's just time. We've discovered that it really helps to give each other a day here and there to get away and just be alone.

Peggy _____

So often neither Don nor I could relate to how the other was feeling. People would say to me, and they still do, "At least you have each other." That was supposed to be comforting, but they just didn't realize how difficult it is to understand the way another person feels grief. A lot of time it caused friction between us, or silence. Sometimes he would be quiet, and he would look like he was hurting. I would wonder what he was thinking about. Should I ask? What would happen then? But I would say nothing.

Sometimes he would go days and days and not say anything. I would feel hurt because I was left out.

It was so hard at first for me to realize how individual a thing grieving is for each person. We need to be sensitive to how the other is grieving — and to when he is. We have to give him the benefit of the doubt.

We felt it so differently. In fact, at times I was embarrassed because I didn't feel as bad as I perceived him to be feeling. There were even times when I thought he would rather I had been the one who died. He seemed to have isolated himself so much that I wished it had been me. I was just sure that Don needed Jacob more than he needed me.

Now I know he just needed time. It wasn't whether he loved me more or the boys more — it was simply his way of handling the hurt. Not realizing what was going on inside him made me feel terribly insecure, and made my own pain more acute. I wish now I had understood — if I had, it would have helped both of us.

Don and I have had to learn to let ourselves be vulnerable with each other, and with the boys, and sometimes as a family unit. Eventually, I saw great beauty in how each of us accepted the other. It made me think of a finely tuned machine working smoothly. It seemed that when Don was hurting the most, I would be stable, and when I was having a rough time, he was able to strengthen me. Our support flowed back and forth. And when either of the boys was struggling, at least one of us had the strength to recognize it and help him move through it. Sometimes the boys would just come and hold us if we were crying. When they were crying, we would hold them. We all gained strength from each other.

One time, several months after Jacob's death, we went to Disneyland. Going there has always been a special time for our family, and we do certain things almost as a ritual. First we go for Mickey Mouse pancakes. Then we go to the Pirates of the Caribbean. After that there are other things we always do in the same order.

This particular time, we did all those things — but we weren't ALL there. I wept openly all day. I didn't cry out, but the tears just kept falling. Everything went along fine and no one showed any reaction. It was as though that was normal for Mom, so it was OK. But a while after we got home, Donny came into our room. With his hands on his hips he said indignantly, "By the way, Mom, the next time we go to Disneyland, I don't want you crying all over the place — because it makes me miserable."

His honesty brought a fresh breeze. His obvious security delighted me. I had been having a tough time, but he was not afraid to let me know that it was ruining his time, too.

We are learning to give the gift of honesty to each other. This may seem like a strange thing to say, but we have learned that grief also is a gift — given by God.

In the Bible, in Matthew 5:4, God says, "Blessed are they that mourn." That means happy. Not a fun-loving, playful, hilarious kind of happy; but rather the deep, peaceful joy that comes with the fulfillment of the accompanying promise — "for they shall be comforted." God Himself has made that promise, and He will keep it.

When first reminded of that lovely beatitude, I confess I didn't feel very blessed. The blessings are there now, though, when I see an old toy of Jacob's, for example, or his favorite booth in a familiar restaurant. The tears still come, but they remind me of the love we shared and the happy times we had.

Feeling so intensely at different times since his death has taught me just how deeply I can love someone, and allowing myself to experience the grief opened me up to the freedom to love again. I can love completely because, even though the person might be taken away from me physically, I now know the love never stops. And that is a warm, comforting, positive, happy thing that I have.

We gain a sense of thorough satisfaction when we realize that within us is created the capacity for those deep feelings. In that way, we have close fellowship with God through the Holy Spirit, because we know from Scriptures that He has deep feelings as well — joy, anger, and even grief.

It was a relief to learn that it's all right to have those intense feelings. I react sometimes now with passing pangs, but no surges of resentment, no boiling anger. The blessing that comes with mourning is a wholesome grief, a sorrow that is as much a part of life as laughter. When the moments of sadness come, tears fill my eyes because of love.

Don _____

Not only am I learning the value of grief, but I'm also discovering a lot about the grieving process. Grief is not a sign of weakness, as some people would have us believe. Rather, it is a normal reaction. And when dealt with, it can be wholesome and good. When we allow ourselves to grieve, we unclog the channels so the comforting can come.

The process of grief involves going through several steps, including shock, denial, guilt, anger, helplessness and hopelessness before acceptance and the ability to resume living finally come. These steps may occur in a predictable order, or they may be all mixed up. It doesn't matter; the comforting will still come if, as they appear, you allow yourself to go through them — and allow God to accompany you.

No one enters into grief knowing all about how to deal with it properly. It's somewhat like parenting. We're all kids who grow up to be parents, and we have to learn as we go, through trial and error. We just know that our first child is going to be the greatest child in the world, because we've seen mistakes others have made and we certainly will not make those mistakes with our kids. The problem is, we make a complete set of our own mistakes and our first child becomes a sort of sacrificial goat on the family altar. But we learn, and with each succeeding child, we grow a little wiser in parenting.

Peggy and I are growing wiser in grieving, and so is our congregation. We had tried to help and support others through their grieving process many times, but this time our people saw their shepherd as the victim. Because he was highly visible, I believe it opened their eyes to a lot of what may have been missed before in the hurting of others, and they became more deeply involved. They have come to realize grieving is not only for the family who's had the loss, but it is also for the members of the church and the community who have lost one of their own, and who now suffer with the family.

That, I believe, is the fellowship Jesus intended, and it is what Paul referred to as *koinonia* (fellowship in the arena of all areas of life — the joy, the peace, the laughter, and also the sorrow). It is not complete until the things our people became aware of are learned. Then it begins moving out from that first circle of people, like a little ripple, and it starts another, and then another. With our church, that understanding of grieving has spread out to other groups, and it keeps spreading. It may not be complete, or perfect, but it's moving in the right direction.

One thing we must be careful of as we all try to understand the process of grief is not to be in a hurry.

Grieving is a slow process, and you have to go through it at your own pace. Sometimes you will see a child who has been pushed into walking too soon, but the child who has been allowed to crawl longer seems to do better later on with his motor skills because of what developed during that crawling period. You can't rush the process. You can hope for it and do everything you can to help it along, but you can't make a child mature faster than he is able. If you try to rush him, his muscular, mental, and physical abilities do not develop together, and he can end up somewhat off balance.

It's the same with the grieving cycle. If you move too fast, you will miss some important lessons you need to learn. If you go from A to C, missing B, you can be sure that when the devil attacks you, he will aim for B. You haven't gone through that stage, and that's where you're most vulnerable, most apt to be knocked off balance.

One of the first things that showed us how easily we could be jarred from a foundation of outer calm happened to Peggy just a couple of weeks after Jacob's death.

All the family had left and she was home alone with Donny and Braxton for the first time. The boys got hungry and asked her to fix them some lunch. Mechanically, she went to the kitchen and fixed their plates as usual.

When she called the boys to eat, Braxton looked at the table and asked, "Mom, who's the third plate for?"

Reality hit her so hard she became nauseated. She couldn't answer Braxton, but just took the plate off and emptied it. She didn't say anything, and the boys didn't say any more, either. Realizing that she had made lunch for Jacob, and he wasn't going to be there to eat anymore, she just broke down and cried.

I really hurt for Peggy at that time. Now I know that God has it all charted. He knew she needed that experience, and He knows how long you need to spend in each area. He is well aware of where you are at any given time. You need to let God, through His Holy Spirit, walk you through it in His own time. He may send people to help you through, but He will not send people to rush you through.

We also must be careful not to let anyone else try to force us into any particular cycle of grieving before we are ready. When we are told by well-meaning people, "Okay, that's enough now. You've cried long enough. It's time to stop," we are being pushed into a mold that we don't fit into. We need to understand the work of grief. We need to be strong enough, and have enough trust in the Lord to help us, so that we can do what is best for us regardless of what someone else says.

People tried at times to walk Peggy and me through certain grieving cycles when we were simply not able to handle them. I'm a compartmentalizer. I like to put an issue into a little cubbyhole and leave it there until I'm ready to deal with it. Sometimes that's within the confines of my own office, where I close the door and cry. To this day, at times I still cry because of the loss, and I cry because I miss Jacob.

I seemed to experience my grief in three basic cycles: tears, denial, and then acceptance. The other things were more or less interwoven with these three main periods.

For example, the first night it rained after Jacob was buried, I went through an emotional upheaval that probably was the most intense point of all my suffering. I thought I had fully accepted his death, but something deep within me still denied its reality.

I began pacing the floor that night, and Peggy asked me what was wrong.

Awash with tears, I choked out, "All I can see is my little boy, all alone on the side of that hill, buried six feet under the ground, and the water is falling . . . and is hitting him . . . and hitting him . . . and I can't do anything to protect him."

I suddenly felt like a caged lion, desperate to get out. "I want to get a shovel and go dig him up and bring him home and put him in our back yard. I'm his father, and I want to protect him."

Peggy just looked at me, her eyes full of understanding. She didn't say a word.

"I know he's dead," I sobbed, "and I know he's buried, and that he's out of my care. But this is . . . I've been hit with something . . . I've never experienced anything like this before, and I can't handle it. I cannot control nature."

There was no way that anyone could have walked me through the anguish I felt, nor could anyone have pushed me through the pain raging inside me. And if I had tried to rush through it, or to ignore it or bypass it, I would have missed a vital part of trusting God.

I wasn't aware of it at the time, but He was working carefully with me through that night. When I tried to analyze it later, I heard God saying to me, "Don, I know how you felt. Remember Calvary? How do you think I felt then? The most difficult thing I ever had to do was turn my back on My Son. No one else will ever understand how I felt. And no one on earth will ever understand how you felt that night when the reality of what happened hit you. But I know. And I know how difficult it was for you. I understand, and now I want you to recognize that you are learning how to trust Me with your feelings."

I suppose that night I experienced a degree of every phase of grieving that there is. I know now that it was a necessary step for me, and, though pain and sadness still come, the pain has never been quite so bad since.

The sadness comes from time to time to all who grieve, and that is normal, but there is something we need to be cautious of. That is the possibility of moving into excessive mourning, which is not normal. When people *choose* to be sorrowful, for whatever reason, that becomes unhealthy mourning. I don't suppose a person ever completely outgrows grief, but when someone finds his identity in the grieving, that can mean trouble.

For example, when you see pictures everywhere, or the loved one's clothing is still in the closet after many months or even years, and the grieving person seems to have no interest in life other than talking about the person he lost, you wonder if the individual isn't experiencing some unhealthy emotions.

Another example is the one who has not been able to deal with the guilt he feels. Feeding the grief and keeping it alive becomes a way of assuaging that guilt. You probably have known someone who expresses deep resentment about a loved one's death many years later. I often wonder just what guilt that person is harboring.

Withdrawal can be another sign of unhealthy grieving. Along with that can come excessive drinking — sometimes privately, sometimes publicly — or overeating. The person who refuses to allow himself to begin living his own life again may be suffering from an acute case of self-pity. Usually this person feels unable to "face the world" or handle the needs of daily living, so he keeps to himself, maybe staying home all the time. In this case comfort and healing just don't come.

Some people are fearful of facing their grief and working through it, and they will deny it or suppress it. They are not sure they could survive if they allowed it to come out. Depression (which, remember, is anger turned inward upon oneself) causes these people to feel hopeless and actually believe they are helpless. And as long as they stay in this state, they really are pretty helpless.

Sometimes the expression of a person's grief must be side-tracked because of family, financial, health, or other pressures.

One young man in his late teens saw his sister killed in an automobile accident. Other lives were in danger, so he snapped into action. He loved his sister greatly, but there was no time for crying, no opportunity to express his inner feelings.

After the initial shock passed, the man went back to college and buried himself in activity. Eventually he graduated and took his place in the business world.

Ten years later, the now thirty-year-old man sat in a jumbo jet, talking casually with his seatmate. Suddenly something triggered a memory of his sister's young, happy face. Oh, how he had loved her! And he dissolved into uncontrollable tears.

The way he had handled his grief earlier had not brought comfort or healing.

A young mother of four children lost her own mother from cancer. Her father could not express his grief, nor could he stand for anyone else to openly express theirs. When the young woman started to cry during the funeral, he stopped her with, "Hey, you can't break down. If you do, whose shoulder am I going to cry on?" He thought he was doing her a favor, but he actually caused her to sidetrack her grief. It was five years before that young woman could allow herself to weep for her mother.

It came about one day when the young woman and her husband had been under extreme financial pressure, and then she became sick. Overwhelmed, she started crying and couldn't stop. She cried for three days until finally, her tears spent, she felt cleansed and relieved. For the first time in five years she was able to love other women — friends, relatives, and co-workers — freely and without fear. She hadn't thought she could survive grief, but discovered she could, and then received the comfort and deep joy of freedom from that fear.

When grief is handled in any of the ways we have just talked about, we cannot experience healing. I have heard it said so often, "Adversity will make you better — or bitter." By putting our faith in God, and following His leading, by doing what we know He wants us to do and letting Him do for us what we can't do for ourselves in our own strength, we can trust Him to make us "better." It is our choice.

True grief will come in cycles, like gigantic waves washing over you, and then it subsides for a while. Sometimes I think it's as though there is a clock inside the grieving person, and as the time ticks by the cycles get longer.

The first couple of months it seems I cried all the time. Then the Lord sort of set the alarm and said, "Okay, you don't need to cry for a while, now, but when the alarm goes off, it will be time again. And when that time comes, you just go ahead and cry." The alarm can take the form of something you see, or something someone says, or it can be a number of things wearing on you, not anything in particular, but the time for a cleansing has come. The alarm goes off again, and God says, "Okay, it's time." And you release the emotions that have been building up.

It's been several years now and I don't need to be crying about this all the time, but at certain times the alarm goes off and I still just flat out weep. The times are getting farther and farther apart but I don't think they will ever stop completely.

One dear lady in our church, who lost her daughter years ago, calls every so often just to talk. She says, "I know how you feel." Her clock is still ticking, and many times the things she says have been just what I needed.

One thing she said was, "In a way you were lucky that Jacob went quickly. For months and months I watched in agony as my daughter died . . . and died . . . and died . . . from that cancer."

We talked about it, and I discovered we had a common ground. It was no different for me at thirty-three to face losing my six-year-old from what it was for her in her sixties to lose her daughter. The pain was just as intense. Even though her daughter had been married and living away from home for more than twenty-five years, she was still hers. The loss was just as real to her, and it still is all these years later. She'll call when she is lonely, and — I think she knows that it's my time, too — my alarm will go off, and we weep into the phone together.

I know the clock is also ticking inside Peggy. Sometimes I look at her and I can tell by her eyes that this is her time. She needs to block everything else out, and, outwardly or inwardly let the tears flow. Her times are different from mine.

Everyone grieves differently, but I'm certain that the clock ticks away inside each heartbroken person, bringing his own times for weeping around. As it does, and as we respond to the alarm, the healing begins to come little by little.

18

The Process of Healing

One of the problems we have when we deal with grief is that we don't want to be *healed* — we want to be *cured.* And there's a big difference.

A person in a wheelchair is not "cured" until he can leap out of the chair and run away from it. But the Lord may be "healing" him on the inside so that he can accept what he is going through with the right attitude. He can reflect, through his circumstances, the love of Jesus and the way that love should be displayed. That's what we are in the process of learning.

When God brings about a cure, it is complete to the point where there is no more evidence of the problem. But the healing that He brings about and that is spoken of in the Bible is in our attitudes and in our lives, and it allows us to accept an irreversible situation.

If you were paralyzed and the Lord cured you, He would have taken away all evidence of your paralysis. Eventually you would forget what it was like to be in a wheel chair.

The healing we have received is not a curing of the pain. Our hearts still ache. For God to bring about a complete cure, He would have to wipe away all memory of Jacob and of the accident. We would be cured of remembering his birthday and wanting other people to remember it. We would not remember any of the things we did together or the secrets we shared. We would even forget what it was like to have Jacob around.

So many people have a "quick-fix" mentality. Uncomfortable in the presence of a suffering person, they want everything to be okay instantly. They want us cured. It would have been great to have had a "quick-fix" because we were constantly in front of people, and we could have walked around with smiles on our faces, saying, "Oh, yes, the Lord has really provided."

But God, in His great wisdom, didn't do that. He has not taken away our memory or our caring. Rather, He is teaching us how to accept what happened and to trust Him to bring about the best from the situation. We have put it all at the foot of the cross and we want Him to receive the glory from whatever our remembering brings.

I see that remembering also in the Bible when Paul speaks of his treatment in Philippi. He and Silas had been beaten and jailed for casting a demon out of a girl and robbing her masters of their income. We don't know how seriously Paul and Silas were injured, and, though they were miraculously released, we don't have any record of whether or not they were cured of their injuries.

Out of experience, though, Paul says, "I thank my God for my every remembrance of you." He has a God-honoring attitude, and he is saying, "Because that happened, and because God was in it, you were brought to the saving knowledge of Jesus Christ."

When God, over a period of time, takes us through the healing process, we move from one point of development to another, and then to another. We see growth in our lives, and we can glorify Him. Ours is not a feet-off-the-ground or head-in-the-clouds faith. Rather than a quick, flashing cure, it is a gradual change, a continual growing right here where we are. Like the warming of the room, it begins long before we feel it or know it's happening.

Recently, a grieving couple who needed to find some understanding came to Peggy and me for counseling. The man asked, "It's been a year now, and we're still crying. Is that normal?"

His wife added, "I still get so weepy. Is that okay?"

We assured them that it certainly was okay and that it was normal. Feelings are not bad or good, they just are. Then I described for them the difference between being cured and being healed.

"You are not *cured* from your loss," I explained. "It is still just as real as it ever was. But your healing is making Heaven more dear to you because you still love your daughter and you know that one day you will be with her again."

The man wiped tears off his cheeks and his wife pulled a handkerchief from her purse.

"Don't try to shut off your crying," I advised. "It's a safety valve for your mind. It provides a healthy release, and the tears will clean out your storehouse of grief."

The man took a deep breath, and asked, "But will we ever be normal, again?"

I waited a moment and then said, "Your healing will be gradual. God is slowly weaning you from the pain, but He allows you the crying times to help you realize just how deep your feelings for your daughter really are and how much more precious Jesus is because she is with Him."

Their obvious struggle in the valley of their grief touched our hearts.

There are some things we can do that will help us move *through* our valley of grief and on toward comfort and healing.

One of those things is to recognize and accept the fact that death is going to come to all of us. It's a part of life.

Our society doesn't want to see it that way. We don't want to face it and we don't want to talk about it. We try to deny its reality. Funeral homes are quiet, beautiful places, softly lit, with soothing music playing, and we visit our loved one in a "slumber room." The physical effects of death on the person's body are camouflaged with make-up, and we dress the body in fine clothing. We add the flowers, our visitors come dressed in their best. Even with all the beauty, though, we feel worse during this time than we ever have before. We try to cover the stark reality of the loss of a life. We try, through a peaceful atmosphere, to escape the mental anguish, yet we sit there in that room, and we suffer.

Even Christians have a hard time with it. We attack it with positive thoughts of the resurrection and of Heaven. We don't want to mourn. Yet Jesus said, "Blessed — happy — are those who mourn." They are the ones who will receive comfort.

One night, some time after Jacob died, Peggy was in need of special comfort. It had been a particularly rough day and she was crying. She had been thinking of him being all alone in Heaven. Oh, he was in the company of grandparents and friends who were already there, but that didn't help. And nothing I could say would stop the torrent of her tears.

"I want to be alone for a while," she sobbed, "just to be able to cry."

We were in the family room, and I said, "I think I'll go on to bed, then. Okay?"

She nodded, and I turned in.

An hour passed. And another. Finally, after about three hours she came to bed.

Her face was still covered with tears, but she was smiling and excited. Stunned, I asked, "What happened?" It was obvious her deep sorrow had somehow been turned to radiant joy.

"Oh, Don," she answered, "it was just wonderful. I was so confused, and felt so bad. Nothing made sense, and I felt silly being so mixed up and worried about Jacob. I've been his mother for a long time, and I felt so responsible. When the kids are hungry I want to feed them, and when they're cold I want to get them a coat, and when they're alone . . . and I saw Jacob so alone . . . I felt sick, physically sick. I was praying and letting God know my heart about all these things, and He came to me, and . . . "

The tears came again and she couldn't talk for a minute, so I waited.

Then she continued, "He gave me a vision of our boy passing from life to death . . . to life! It seemed He said to me, 'Peggy, I want to calm your fears and let you see what happened to *our* precious little Jacob.'

"With that He pulled back the curtain and I could see Jacob walking through the 'valley of the shadow of death.' Darkness was all around him as he walked, but then it began getting lighter and yet lighter, until finally Jacob stopped — and he was standing completely in the light. He was looking all around at his new surroundings, when I saw a man coming in his direction. When Jacob caught sight of him, he began to run toward him, shouting, 'Jesus!' At the same time, Jesus ran toward him calling, 'Jacob.'

"Don, I saw our Gentle Shepherd pick up our precious child and smother him with hugs and kisses. I really knew then that He is the 'God of Jacob.'

"I'm so relieved. I feel so good about it because I know my little boy is not alone, and he never will be. I don't have to worry about him any more. His Jesus loves him and He will take better care of him than I ever could."

Though it didn't take away all our sadness or grief, that vision of Peggy's brought both of us a great deal of comfort and made his death infinitely more acceptable for us. We realized that it wasn't hopeless, nor was it the end of all things for our lives.

When we accept death as a part of life, the next logical step is to accept our grief as normal. This will lessen the confusion in our minds over what is happening. If death is a natural part of life, then the grief that accompanies it is also natural. Accepting the grief and allowing ourselves to express it results in the quickest and most effective healing possible.

Realizing the normalcy of grief shows us that God allows these things to happen, and that helps us to leave the past behind and actually be about the business of rebuilding our lives. With God in control, calamities can be turned into challenges, endings can become beginnings — and the peace will come. God does not allow us to be separated from our loved ones for no purpose. We have a job to do, and with His help, it can be done.

Long ago, David, the king of Israel, recognized these truths. He had sinned with Bathsheba, and God's judgment on him was that he would lose his son. David's grief was deep during the child's illness. He fasted and wept before God. I can picture him face down on the dirt, sobbing and begging the Lord to spare his little boy. He could find no comfort.

Then the child died, and the elders were afraid to tell David. As much as he was grieving before, what would he do now? He surely would be inconsolable.

When David saw the men whispering, he sensed that the end had come. "Is the child dead?" he asked.

"He is dead," they answered, trembling.

David's acceptance of God's truth was immediately evident. He got up, washed and anointed himself, changed his clothes, and went to the tabernacle to worship God. Afterward, he went home, and the elders, astonished, finally got up the courage to speak to him. "We don't understand," they said. "While the child was alive, you fasted and wept; but when the child died, you rose and ate food."

"He's dead. Why should I fast? Can I bring him back again? I shall go to him, but he will not return to me" (2 Samuel 12:15-23).

One of the most important steps toward healing is committing ourselves and our entire lives to the Lord for His purpose, and David's commitment to God had steered him directly onto the path of healing.

Making that commitment our primary goal in life assures us His peace and support as we need it through whatever lies ahead. We can begin to rebuild our lives on the foundation of His love, and that frees us to be ourselves. To be real. We have no need to put on any kind of false front.

Actually, in light of the immediate commitments Peggy and I made to each other and to God, it would have been pretty hard for us not to be real. The strength of our commitments seemed to grow through the months.

In effect, we immediately rededicated our lives to the Lord when Jacob died. Some of the people around us blamed God instead of looking to Him for strength, but we simply shared our prayers and verbally recommitted our lives to His service. We said, "This is not going to shake us in what we're doing. Rather, it's going to reaffirm our testimony to the truth of the Scripture that says where your treasure is, that's where your heart is."

Our hearts, our desires, were now for heavenly things because we had treasure planted there. So our recommitment was partly to make sure, to the best of our ability, that our relationship with Heaven would be the priority of our lives.

We also reaffirmed our commitment to each other and to our marriage vows. That special moment was an extremely emotional time for us both.

I sometimes think that in one sense, Jacob had a choice to make, and that was whether to stay or to go. The depth of our commitment to each other might depend on his decision. If he stayed, we might get things out of perspective. We might allow our kids to become so important to us that we would miss our commitments to each other, or to the Lord. If he would go, we would be faced with making different choices, and with sealing our commitments. Our choices might not be just right, but we would have to stick to them. We sometimes wonder now, if Jacob had not died, would we be as close to each other and to the Lord as we are? To us that seems a significant part of what we were to learn from his death.

Since that time, we have talked a lot of things out, and we've had a chance to put things into proper perspective. Our commitments to each other became more and more important, and we determined that, through our marriage and our lives together, we would try to show that you don't have to succumb to the pressures that hit you with the death of a child. Through it all we would work things out because our goal was to see our boy again one day in

Heaven, and we intended to see him together. We were not going to be a split family.

I think that was one of the main things we really were aiming for in the renewing of our commitments. We became more conscious of our decision in the days immediately following when we were barraged by the statistics. Some people seemed overly concerned about the threat to our marriage, and, in a way, that served to strengthen us because we were determined to show them that it would not be true for us. And we knew the only way we could make it was to find our strength in the Lord and in each other. Many times we have talked about the fact that we just have one another. When I need strength, Peggy's my strength, and when she needs it, I'm her strength. We just knew we couldn't allow any of the things that come up to affect our relationship.

Sometimes when we go to the graveside we remember what we said to one another and the promises we made to God. We said, "Our lives are Yours—You can do what You want with us. It's solely up to You. If You want us to go somewhere else, we'll go. If You want us to stay here, we'll stay. If You want us to have good things, we'll have them, but if we go through tough times, we will still serve You."

I became a great lover of Job as I understood the trials he went through. I appreciated the fact that he still could say, "Though He slay me, yet will I serve Him," and, "I know that my redeemer liveth."

I increasingly recognized the depth of my commitment. I was basically saying, "Lord, everything that I have, I surrender to You. I don't want control of my life anymore because I tend to foul things up. I want to walk in Your steps. I want to be able to say like Paul, 'Be ye followers of me.'"

Walking in His steps, serving Him, sometimes means we must do our part to promote healing for ourselves, and for others. The time came when we had to take things into our own hands for Braxton.

He had been living for a year in Jacob's shadow, and that can be a hard thing for a boy to bear. Jacob began to be larger than life and it was overshadowing Braxton. The bigger Jacob became, the more Braxton withdrew.

Because I felt Jacob's loss so keenly, I had been afraid I might portray the wrong thing to Braxton so I had tried to be careful. Jacob was no more important to me than Braxton — just different. It was never our intention, or anybody else's, that Jacob take on that dimension. But it happened. So we eventually had to act.

We planned a specific family time for that purpose, and I began to reassure Braxton, "This is a special day for us and I want you to know something. Your brother was loved by a lot of people — he was a special child — but he was no more special than you are. You may not fully understand now, but one day you'll know how deeply Mommy and Daddy felt about losing Jacob. When you have children of your own, you will realize how precious each one is and that you don't love any one more than any other. When one child is sick or hurt, he tends to get more attention than the others — but he is not loved any more than they are. If Jacob seems to appear more important to us than you, it's just that he isn't with us any more."

Braxton asked, "Do you still love him?"

"Yes, Braxton," I answered. "We love Jacob very much. But we love you every bit as much as we do him. We want you to know that, and to remember it.

"We've set this time aside for you to let you know how special you are to us. We can't make up for the past year, and we really don't want to, because it has been a growing process for all of us. But now we're going on from here, together, as a family.

"We are not going to bury Jacob in the sense that we will never mention him again. He is still just as much a part of our family as he was when he was here. We're not going to forget him, and we don't want you to forget him, either. We are going to talk about him together, but it will be in a positive way, because he's not that much different from you two boys. "

"As you grow older," Peggy added, "you'll probably find that we'll forget some of the bad things Jacob did. It'll be the same as when you get older and we forget some of the things you've done."

That talk seemed to help Braxton accept the situation and gain more confidence in himself and in his position with us, and it brought Jacob back down to the size he really was.

That experience not only relieved some of Braxton's pain, it brought increased healing for all of us.

Another area that can be particularly painful is in the negative feelings brought about by useless platitudes of well-meaning friends. You will know you are making progress in healing when you can rise above their remarks. It's impossible to find relief in those empty words, yet we tend to feel guilty when we are not consoled by them.

How often do we hear things like these?

"Well, she's with the Lord."

"He's out of his misery."

"You'll be together again someday."

"God will supply your needs."

A friend who lost her little boy was suffering bravely, though her heart was broken. She received a note one day that read, "You're probably rejoicing now because you know that your son is in Heaven. And, after all, you have three others!"

Rejoicing?

"I didn't feel any rejoicing at all," she told me bitterly. When these kinds of things are said to us, we hate to frustrate our comforters, but we don't feel a bit better for all their 'sage' words – and our guilt deepens.

Grief, when it is fresh and heavy, can stop our ears, even to the words of the Bible. People don't know what to say to us, but they want to say something, so they often quote an inappropriate Scripture or say the wrong thing. It's awkward for them. Maybe they don't phrase it right, and maybe we only hear the words. But when we have time to think it through, we usually can figure out what they were trying to say.

If this has happened to you, take heart. Eventually you will realize these people really do want to help, and you won't resent them for saying what they do. When that time comes, you will know that healing is taking place.

Another effective step you can take toward your own healing is to reach out when you are hurting. No one is a mind reader, and others want to help, and people are more available than we might think. When a person you trust asks, "How are you today?" be honest. Admit that you're feeling down, and let that person help you.

Some things you can do to make it easier for others to give you the help you need include:

Let them know when you have physical needs. If you have too much to do and not enough time or energy, or if you're too depressed or ill to manage, ask for help with one of the tasks.

Ask for a talking time. Pick a person you trust and let that person know that you don't need advice particularly, but you just need someone to listen. And then talk.

Write out your feelings to someone who loves you. Sit down and write that person a letter. Pour your heart out. They, and you, will be glad you did.

Ask someone to read to you, especially from the Bible. You can even pick the Scripture you'd like if you're up to it. If not, let the other person choose. Listen carefully, and let the words minister to you.

Let someone know when you need a hug. One woman, when asked how she was doing, answered, "I'm running low on hugs." Her friend bought her a blue T-shirt with a fat little cartoon character on it saying, "Gimme a hug." She wore it once a week, and said many of her friends enjoyed giving her a therapeutic hug.

Ask someone to pray with you, or for you — right then. Most Christians would like to pray with a hurting friend, but will not suggest it themselves lest they "remind" their friend of the hurt.

If you think about it, other ideas may come to you as well. We were meant to grieve — but not as those who have no hope. God often offers hope to us through others of His children.

Death is a funny thing. Years down the road, it still affects you. I know of people who have no hope, who have not been able to settle their questions, and who cannot function because they lost someone close to them and have not been able to accept the fact. God really is in control and you can't change the things that happen. People are born, and people die. You can't change what is a part of life. But there comes a time to turn it over to God. We must realize that our loved one is God's child, and the sooner we recognize that and allow God to have His child, the sooner we begin to get things into focus again for ourselves.

For Peggy and me, understanding that Jacob is really God's son lifted a lot of pressure. We realized that God knows the beginning and He knows the end, and He knows the time we will spend on this earth. He also knows the things that we will never be able to change. We were able to say, "God, we know that these things work according to Your plan and purpose, and we submit to that."

We understood that God, who takes care of everything, is taking personal care of our son, too. That relieved us of the guilt we were feeling about: Why did we let the kids go to San Diego? Did we just want to get rid of them for the week? Maybe we just selfishly wanted a vacation — was it because of our selfishness that our son died?

When we accepted that God is in control, we were able to, as Peter says, "cast all your doubt [your fears, your cares] on Him, for He careth for you." No one is going to care for Jacob like my Father, and no one is going to care for me like He will. There is not one arrow that will pierce my soul that will not first pass through His heart, and my child will not experience any hurt that He has not experienced first. He knows . . . and He cares.

There is no question about Jacob being God's son. He was, and still is. That's been settled. Knowing that brings us consolation and revives our hope. We hold on to that, and we face today, and we look forward to tomorrow.

19

A New Perspective

*Peggy*_____

I had been drowning in an ocean of pain and sorrow, and then I climbed into a lifeboat. The pain still rocked the boat, but I looked out over it all and began to see a new perspective. I could say, "Okay, I'm still feeling it; I'm still tossing, but I'm secure. I think I can be comfortable."

Today, that new perspective allows me to think about how much Jacob enjoyed the time he had. It has helped me take another look at each of my two remaining children, our lives together as a family, and my own life.

Before, when we went places and did things together, we had a lot of fun, and we were important to one another, but we were self-centered. Now my thoughts have expanded, and I notice other things around me. I stop . . . I literally stop . . . and admire a tree, the mountains, or a clear blue sky. Seeing the importance of some things makes it easier to let go of others.

I was a person who always had to have something to look forward to. I'm not that way so much any more. I look

228

at Jacob's death, a focal point for me, and I say, "He didn't have enough time to enjoy all that I think he would have wanted to," and I want my other children to have that opportunity. I want to help them make each day special because I don't know how long we will have together. I hadn't been conscious before of making sure that my children enjoyed their everyday experiences and noticed little things. Now I am very conscious of it.

Life is forever; *here* is not forever. We know that in theory, but in reality we believe we will live to be a hundred. We need to be aware that that's not necessarily true, and we need to enjoy one another and what God has placed here for us. Today. Now. Like Jacob did.

The memories are sweet. Sometimes they hurt, but they also help me keep that new perspective.

Don _____

I think a loss, such as we have had, develops and matures a person, but sometimes you have to move further away to see a thing more clearly. The closer you are to something, the harder it is to get a good overall perspective of it.

For example, imagine a husband and wife arguing. They are in close proximity, and it gets difficult for them. Then one of them — the husband, say — takes a copper teapot and sets it on a table. He says, "Okay, instead of you or me being the problem, let's put the problem here, in this teapot on the table. Let's not talk about you and me for a while; let's talk just about the problem."

The farther away from themselves that the man and wife can move the teapot, or problem, the more impersonal it becomes and the easier it is to deal with.

Grieving is somewhat like that. At first, you're so wrapped up in your loss that it's hard to understand anybody else's loss. Because grieving hits people differently, each one needs a new perspective. By moving away from it, you can see it in a different light and get that fresh outlook. That's development.

Of course, hindsight helps, too.

And there is no hurry. You have years to reflect on the loss, on what you had with him, and on what you will have because of where that person is now.

The first year the certainty of Jacob being in Heaven was positive. It was settled. Yet, even though you're sure he's there, you sometimes have to make yourself accept it by saying things to yourself like, "I know he's in Heaven. I know one day we're going to be there with him." Your mind knows you will be reunited, but it takes time to convince your inner self that it actually will happen.

Then in the second year the doubts begin. The devil starts throwing arrows at your convictions. I think everybody who loses a loved one has some doubts about the whole concept of Heaven. Is it really real? Or are we just kidding ourselves?

You know it's real, but the enemy puts pressure on you. If you're a Christian, yes, you believe in Heaven and you assign your loved one to a place there because he's yours and you love him. Yes, you know he's in the presence of Jesus. Otherwise the separation of death has no validity. But the enemy wants to destroy your most prized certainty.

I was more frustrated during that year than at any other time. I could see no form of equity or fairness. I don't mean to say we were all that righteous, but we were trying to do what was right. And then one thing after another, after another . . .

Peggy had surgery, Jacob died, then Peggy got sick again and was sick for so long, then I had the car accident that brought about ten months of real physical suffering before I had the back operation. Along with all this I struggled with how to help the boys. It seemed that everything I tried to do took us straight into a roadblock of some kind. Then a year after Jacob's death we let that family stay in our home while we were away and the little boy got hurt and they sued us for negligence. Braxton got a virus in his hip bone that looked like it might destroy the hip itself—his leg would never have grown and he wouldn't have been able to walk. He was in bed and whenever he needed to go anywhere we had to pick him up and carry him. We also were involved with insurance companies regarding Jacob's death, and with lawyers regarding the suit . . .

We finally assumed one of two things must be true: Either we were the worst people in the whole world, or the devil had turned his big guns on us to challenge us while people around us watched.

Then I remembered a story I tell once in a while at the church.

In pre-Civil War days a Southern man and his slave went hunting together one day. While they were out, the slave said to his master, "You know, I been havin' some turrible dreams lately."

The master asked, "What kind of dreams? Tell me about them."

The slave answered, "Well, someone starts a-chasin' me, and I sees that it's the devil. He yells at me, and cotches me and starts beatin' up on me somethin' fierce."

"You must be an awfully bad man," the master replied, "for the devil to be after you like that. He's never after me; you must be really wicked."

The servant thought a minute, then said to his master, "You tells me that sometimes when you shoots up in the air at the ducks, you hits two—you kills one and you wounds one. When that happens, which one does you go after?"

"That's simple. I go after the one that's wounded. The one that's dead I don't have to bother about."

"Maybe the devil's been tryin' to tell you somethin'," the slave said. "Maybe you be dead—maybe I be jus' wounded."

I felt we had been wounded, and the devil knew that and so that's when he turned the guns on us.

At the same time, though I wouldn't say I felt privileged, I did feel that God had entrusted us with a great deal. The Bible promises He will never give us any more than we can bear, so He must have felt we were capable of living through all those things, difficult as they were.

One of the most frustrating things for me was feeling the pull of what was happening with my family, and also knowing that all those other eyes were looking at us. I felt people wanted to know how we'd react, if we'd pretend it hadn't happened. I believed they wanted to know how we were feeling, so sometimes we would share bits and pieces of ourselves. Some of the folks were kind enough to look at the pieces and appreciate our situation; I felt others, like vultures, picked the pieces apart and fed themselves. They couldn't understand that our being open and sharing how we felt was not just a catharsis for us, but also so they would know that when something happened that might make them feel that way, it would be all right.

My main frustration was in trying to locate the fine line. When the insurance man who represents the other people calls, and instead of saying, "We're sorry your son was killed," he says, "We want to know where the bike is," how do you respond?

He knew I was a pastor. I'd like to have said, "I'm not anybody. Here's how I feel, okay Buddy?"

But can I be myself and let my natural indignation show? Or do I ruin the testimony of being a pastor? And what about eternity? What's most important?

That's where I could see the guns pointing at me. It was a crucial issue. I had every right to be a father, yet I had the responsibility of being a pastor, too. Those were rough times.

By the third year, though, I discovered that I didn't have to assure myself that Jacob was in Heaven, and I didn't have to deal with doubts anymore. The Book of Hebrews says, "Faith is the substance of things hoped for, the evidence of things not seen." Evidence is always based upon fact, and fact is based upon things that you can prove.

From Genesis to Revelation you find a God who cannot lie, who shows you example after example of His faithfulness and ability to keep His word, and pretty soon you don't have to prove that anymore, to yourself or to anybody else. The enemy can say whatever he wants to you, but it doesn't matter. God's track record is good, and you don't have to defend it. The truth of God is not even questionable.

The fourth year, and since then, things have been pretty much the same. The settled certainty is always there.

It's still easy for us to cry over Jacob and our loss, of course. When we talk about it, it seems as though it happened just yesterday. I still ask myself, "Was there anything I could have done that I didn't do?" Every time I read in the newspaper about a child who was in a serious accident, and was put on a life-support system, and then made a miraculous recovery, I wonder. I don't know how badly the child was hurt, and I really do know the answer to our questions, but those times continue to crop up.

When they do, I feel sorrow, but have no regrets. As a parent, I couldn't have done any more for Jacob. I can't say we should have taken him to the House of God more, because he was there all the time. I couldn't say we wish we had been more Christ-like in the home, because we were as Christ-like as we knew how to be. We didn't feel the children were deprived of anything. We had made a commitment to God, and we honored it. And at the hospital, there is not one thing we did that I would change.

We can't ignore the accident, though, or pretend it never happened. We encourage our boys to talk about it and about Jacob. We still celebrate his birthday. We talk about what he might have been at the stage of life he would have reached by now. We re-emphasize to the boys how much their brother loved them. Memories sometimes dim as years go by, and I don't want them to forget the relationship they had.

We talk about the good things that have come out of his death, like the people who received his kidneys and his corneas. Though we highlight the positive things, we are still subject to hurts, but we deal with them as they come. We don't ignore the negative things.

We also talk over the fact that Jacob may have made a mistake. What if he hadn't been riding the bike? Some of the things we deal with as a family are productive for us. We don't let each other sing the blues about it, but we talk about the reality of what happened. We discuss the effect of some mistakes that were made.

We do not minimize the boys' feelings. We treat the boys as people; we never say, "Well, you're young. You'll get over it." We know that they have some of the same feelings we do, and possibly they are even more intense for them.

Sometimes one of the boys will say, "I don't understand . . . "

And one of us will respond by asking, "What don't you understand? What are you struggling with?"

Sometimes we cry. They know how special each of them is to us. They see how much we still love Jacob.

When I have a rough day, it's as though the alarm on the clock I mentioned earlier goes off and God says, "Okay, it's time for you to just let out a few things." It's not usually sadness, though. Sometimes I cry pure tears of joy because I remember how special certain moments were for Jacob. I think, *I'm in good hands with Jesus;* or, *Be patient with me; God isn't finished with me yet;* and I let the tears flow. There is a sense of loss, but I also thank God for my every remembrance of Jacob. It's almost like holy ground to me as I reflect on God's goodness in allowing me those precious memories.

I have to deal with the loss again sometimes on Sunday mornings. Sitting on the platform, or standing in the pulpit, I look out at the congregation, and I don't see Jacob. I do see all those people who knew and loved him, and the tears suddenly well up inside. Everyone out there thinks everything is all right, but I'm dying inside because I miss him so much. Those feelings don't last long, but they do let me know that the healing process is still going on, and I've still got a way to go before I'm completely free of the hurt. Some of the people still go and put flowers on Jacob's grave. Knowing they do that helps our healing, and we talk about how important it is to us that he continues to mean so much to them.

In all honesty, I also have to say that sometimes I have resented God for taking my little boy, although I know that at those times I have been selfish. I don't think I've watched a baseball game where I've been able to just sit and enjoy it without thinking about Jacob and where he would be at this point in his life. That's tough.

Over time, God has changed my perspective. Now, instead of saying, "Where was God?" I am thankful He gave us the privilege of being a part of Jacob's life and having him as a part of ours. I can hardly wait until our lives are joined together again. I have a completely different outlook because the healing, the balm of Gilead, has come and ministered to our need. What's left is no longer a scab that can be pulled off, leaving bleeding, sore tissue underneath; now it's a scar, the visible evidence of the hurt we experienced, but for the most part the tissue is healed.

For example, I can understand now why people don't go to a cemetery after a loved one has been dead for a while. At first you go out continually, then all of a sudden you don't want to go anymore because your visits are so painful. But if you can walk through the experience to the day when you can say, "Okay, I do grieve for that loss," you can deal with it on that basis, and you will see the growth.

For me now, it's not so much a matter of pain, it's just that the house Jacob occupied is located there. He's not there but we go to take care of some business about his house.

Going to the cemetery has made the loss more real to me. Just being where he is buried usually brings a fresh flow of tears. Yet they're not always all sad; usually they're a tribute to happy moments in our lives. The pain comes from knowing I won't have those times with him again here. That's what I have to accept daily.

Today I have done that; I have accepted Jacob's death. I haven't accepted it tomorrow. I have victory over today;

I don't have it over tomorrow. Every day is a new day, and every situation a potential hazard, which can leave a scar.

When I was two years old, one day was particularly hazardous for me. I was in the back of a car my uncle was driving when another driver forced him off the road. He lost control of the car and I came flying down and hit the edge of an open coffee can on the floor. My face was cut from the top of my head down to my throat.

It left a long scar on the side of my face and of course it changed my life. As I grew up, people never realized how deeply the things they said hurt me. For example, sometimes at Halloween the neighbor kids would say things like, "We know what you will be because you already have your mask on."

It was always difficult for me to tell anyone how I felt inside because I wasn't sure they would understand. I wondered if they were laughing at me, or if they would say to me, "That's silly. You shouldn't feel that way."

Falling on the coffee can was something I had no control over, but I suffered the repercussions of it, and it led to a lonely existence. When I looked in a mirror, I saw myself different from the way other people saw me — uglier — so for the most part I kept to myself.

I was fearful of God, and I resented Him for allowing that to happen. I couldn't trust Him. I was not able to get over those feelings for a long, long time, but finally, while in college, I could deal with the fact of that scar and resolve those negative feelings about God.

My experience was the reason I was so concerned about Braxton's feelings. He had no control over Jacob's death, either, and I didn't want him to suffer for years like I did. I'm still watchful over him — I want to help him whenever he needs it.

Although most people don't even notice my scar today, the hurt from those childhood taunts helped make me what I am. Not too long ago I was asked if I'd like to have a plastic surgeon remove the scar. I said, "No, that scar was a part of shaping the kind of person I am. Anyway, it's become so much a part of me I'm not even aware of it anymore."

It's like that with Jacob. His death has left a scar, evidence of my deep suffering, but now it's a part of me. It's not always visible, but God has allowed Peggy and me, and even Braxton and Donny, the opportunity of carrying this scar without all of the bad effects of a visible, physical scar. It's there, and we know it's there, but when we look we really don't see it. It's helping to form us into the people God wants us to be, and it has not become a chip on anyone's shoulder.

One especially important thing to note while waiting for healing to come and scar tissue to form, is that God has a tendency not to do things in a great, grand way. Rather, He generally works in simple ways, through small things that go on around you all the time. And if you're not careful, you'll miss them. If you're not looking, you may not recognize His hand upon your life or the changes He brings about. As I mentioned before, I struggled with that as a pastor for a while, and now I see it in people all the time. They are looking for miracles, big signs and wonders, a loud voice — and those things just don't happen much.

God says through the psalmist, "Be still and know that I am God."

If I have learned anything through knowing who God is, and walking with Him through these experiences, it is that a lot of things happen that I wouldn't have been aware of had I not first been honest with God and told

Him how I felt and what I needed. God rearranges little things to help us.

When I spoke of Jacob before as the grain of wheat, I was much aware that he had a natural magnetism which attracted people to him. They were captivated by his smile and his actions, and those who knew him loved him. After he died I soon realized that those things didn't die with him. They were released in a greater depth, and people still see Jacob when they see Donny. His smile, or something he does, will prompt them to say, "He reminds me so much of Jacob."

Jacob lives on for those people. Sometimes I think that what they remember about him is far greater than what he really was, but his little life did touch them and they learned. One thing I recognized along the way is that it's not only the quantity of time but also the quality of the time one gives, and that the quality lives on after the breaking of the outer shell.

I don't just remember that he was good in sports, but I also remember that he really loved the Lord, and he loved this church, and he loved the people. He was committed to certain things, and I think some people seriously ask themselves, "If a six-year-old can be that committed, why can't I as an adult, who is supposed to see things on a wider spectrum and more in depth than a child does, why can't I be that committed?"

One thing the Lord has taught me is that the fruit of Jacob's life and death is just beginning. All the lessons Peggy and I have already learned are so precious to us, but this is one of the most important to me:

Robert Murray McCheyne, the great Scottish preacher, once said, "Live in such a way that you're missed when you're gone."

I don't want anyone to forget Jacob, but I have found out that he *did* live in such a way that he *would* be missed. Not one week goes by that Jacob's story doesn't touch someone and put new hope in their lives. Whether it's salvation, a new sense of commitment, or just knowing that in each trial a person goes through God is able to provide the needs, Jacob's life is still bearing fruit today.

Somewhere along the way God rearranged some little things to bring to me the realization that He didn't just pluck Jacob up; rather He transplanted him, and now Jacob is growing somewhere else.

I will continue to ask God every day, "Lord, let me see the harvest of Jacob's life."

Full of life.

A Tribute to Jacob

A few days after Jacob died, I called Bill Gray, his baseball instructor, to let him know what had happened. He expressed his condolences and then we talked for a few moments about Jacob's love for baseball. A few days later, I received a letter from Mr. Gray, which said:

Dear Mr. Gregg:

I was most surprised and depressed when you called me the other day regarding your son, Jacob. Having served as his instructor at both our San Diego and Hemet baseball schools, I became very close to him. He had such great enthusiasm and he was such a great boy to be around, that I would have taken him home with me if you would have let me.

Although he was only six years of age, he was the most talented young baseball player I have ever seen. With his talent, enthusiasm and attitude, I figured he would no doubt be a professional baseball player some day. Over the years I have seen many thousands of young ball players, but I have never seen one with his ability at six years of age.

Very truly yours,